THE CASSELL INTRODUCTIONS TO MODERN ENGLISH LITERATURE FOR STUDENTS OF ENGLISH

Modern Poetry

Alex Martin and Robert Hill

CASSELL

Cassell Publishers Limited
Villiers House
41/47 Strand
London WC2N 5JE

First Published 1991

British Library Cataloguing in Publication Data
Modern poetry. — (The Cassell introductions to modern English
literature)
1. Poetry in English, 1900. — Bibliographies
I. Martin, Alex   II. Hill, Robert
821.91208

ISBN 0304 33007 8

This book is affectionately dedicated to
Kenneth Grose and Sydney Bolt.

n by Derek Lee
tions by Taurus Graphics
tting by Litho Link Ltd, Welshpool, Powys, Wales
and bound in Great Britain by Page Bros., Norwich

Acknowledgements

The Editors and Publishers would like to thank the following for their kind permission to reproduce these poems and extracts:

Collins Publishers for 'Children's Song' by R S Thomas; Robson Books Ltd for 'Dead Dog' and 'Incendiary' both from *New and Collected Poems* by Vernon Scannell; John Johnson (Author's Agent) Ltd, London, for 'Warning' copyright Jenny Joseph, from *Rose in the Afternoon*, Dent, 1974; Gallery Press for 'Sonnet for the Class of '58' by James Simmons; Faber and Faber Ltd for 'Liu Ch'e', 'The Jewel Stairs' Grievance' and Note printed beneath, 'Fan-piece, for her Imperial Lord', 'Image from D'Orleans', all from *Collected Shorter Poems* by Ezra Pound; 'Preludes' from *Collected Poems 1909-1962* by T S Eliot; 'The Whitsun Weddings' from *The Whitsun Weddings* and a short extract from 'Single-handed and untrained' from *Required Writing*, both by Philip Larkin; Harcourt Brace Jovanovich, Inc. for 'Fog' and 'Chicago Poem' from *Chicago Poems* by Carl Sandburg, copyright 1916 by Holt, Rinehart and Winston, Inc. and renewed 1944 by Carl Sandburg, reprinted by permission of Harcourt Brace Jovanovich, Inc.; Rosica Colin Ltd for 'Evening' and a short extract from 'London (May 1915)' by Richard Aldington, © Madame Guillaume; Oxford University Press for permission to reprint 'Mort aux Chats' from Peter Porter's *Collected Poems 1983* and 'Sindhi Woman' from *Out of Bounds* by Jon Stallworthy (1963); The Society of Authors as the literary representative of the Estate of John Masefield for 'C.L.M.' by John Masefield; Laurence Pollinger Limited and New Directions for 'The Mutes' by Denise Levertov, 'Hubert's Museum' from *Searching for the Ox* by Louis Simpson (William Morrow & Co. Inc.); 'Money-Madness' and 'We Die Together' by D H Lawrence (Laurence Pollinger Ltd and the Estate of Mrs. Frieda Lawrence Ravagli; Bloodaxe Books for 'Daphne Morse' and 'When You Died' both by Pamela Gillilan from *That Winter* (1986), also for 'Man of Sorrows' by Steve Ellis from *Home and Away* (1987); Anthony Sheil Associates for 'Not Adlestrop' by Daniel Abse, copyright Dannie Abse 1977, 1989; Ellen C. Masters for 'Seth Compton' from *The Spoon River Anthology* by Edgar Lee Masters, published by the Macmillan Company, New York; David Higham Associates Limited for 'To a Poet a Thousand Years Hence' by John Heath-Stubbs from *Selected Poems* published by Carcanet; John Murray (Publishers) Ltd. for 'In Westminster Abbey' from *Collected Poems* by John Betjeman; Random Century Limited for 'Agony Calories' from *Poems 1974-83* by Kit Wright; John Whitworth for 'Max's Verse', copyright John

Whitworth; James MacGibbon (Executor) for 'O Happy Dogs of England' from *The Collected Poems* of Stevie Smith (Penguin) Modern Classics); Weidenfeld & Nicolson and the Executor, Richard Percival Graves for 'A Twin of Sleep' by Robert Graves; Rogers, Coleridge & White Ltd for an extract from *A Book of Train Journeys* by Ludovic Kennedy, published by Rawson, Wade, Inc. New York; Andre Deutsch Ltd for definitions of 'irony' and 'satire' from *A Dictionary of Literary Terms* by J A Cuddon; A M Heath for an extract from *How Children Learn* by John Holt (Penguin Books); Longman Group UK for definitions from the *Longman Active Study Dictionary* and *Longman Dictionary of Contemporary English*; Penguin Books Ltd for extracts from *Fish Cookery* by Jane Grigson (Penguin Books/ Rainbird, 1975) ©Jane Grigson; Random Century Group for entry for 'Moon' from *Hutchinson Encyclopaedia*; World Book Inc. for the article 'Chicago', excerpted from The World Book Encyclopedia. © 1990 World Book, Inc. by permission of the publisher.

We are grateful, too, to the following for permission to produce pictures:

The Board of Trustees of the V & A for *Sark Girl* by Guy Malet, *Au Clair de la Lune* by Ethel Gabain and *The National Gallery* by Stanley Anderson; Hulton-Deutsch for *The Forgotten Gorbals* by Bert Hardy, also for *Pearly King and Queen, Lady Astor, ATS Girl* and *Making a Bomb*; Jonathan Eastland for *Off Wall Street*; the Bodleian Library, Oxford for 'Glory of Life' from *The Wood Engravings of Robert Gibbings* (original illustration from *Glory of Life* by Llewelyn Powys, Golden Cockerel Press 1934); The Ashmolean Museum, Oxford for *Viba* by Gerald Brockhurst; *The Guardian* for *Ribblehead Viaduct* and *Orchestra of the Golden Age*, both by Denis Thorpe; the Illustrated London News for *Accident at Staplehurst in which Charles Dickens was involved*; Mary Evans Picture Library for *Railway car at night* and *Pullman dining car of the 1870s*; London Features International for *Bo Diddley*; Simon Brett for *Cats and Geraniums* by Clifford Webb, © Clifford Webb; Magnum Photos Paris for *Rue Mouffetard* (1959) by Marc Riboud; Sanford J. Greenburger Associates Inc, New York for *Hausherr* from *Ecce Homo* by George Grosz (Dover Publications Inc, New York, 1976)

While every attempt has been made to trace copyright owners, the Publishers would be pleased to hear from any other parties who feel they hold rights to any of the material that has been included.

Our thanks to Robert Peett and Dr Harry Dickinson for advice on pictures, UTS Oxford Centre for allowing us to test some of this material in their classes, and special thanks to Steve McDonald for his valuable help in the initial stages. Our thanks also to our editors, Valerie Elliston and Louise Woods for their lively interest and many helpful suggestions.

Contents

Language Practice: reported speech.
Vocabulary: relationships; words for noises.

6 Trains

Edward Thomas, *Adlestrop*
Philip Larkin, *The Whitsun Weddings*
Steve Ellis, *Man of Sorrows*
Dannie Abse, *Not Adlestrop*

Language Practice: talking about time.
Vocabulary: verbs of motion, gesture and action.

7 Culture

Edgar Lee Masters, *Seth Compton*
Louis Simpson, *Hubert's Museum*
John Heath-Stubbs, *To a Poet a Thousand Years Hence*

Language Practice: relative clauses.
Vocabulary: talking about art and culture; deriving nouns from adjectives.

8 Satire

John Betjeman, *In Westminster Abbey*
Kit Wright, *Agony Calories*
D H Lawrence, *Money-Madness*

Focus on Irony.
Language Practice: interpretation – *you can tell/you know that by . . .;
this suggests/means/shows . . .*
Vocabulary: cooking and food.

9 Cats and dogs

John Whitworth, *Max's Verse*
Peter Porter, *Mort aux Chats*
Stevie Smith, *O Happy Dogs of England*

Language Practice: the language of disapproval.
Vocabulary: choosing the right dictionary definition; derivatives.

10 City life

Carl Sandburg, *Chicago*
Lew Welch, *Chicago Poem*
D H Lawrence, *We Die Together*

Language Practice: uses of *can, can't, could, couldn't.*
Vocabulary: synonyms, definitions and paraphrases.

Key

Introduction

1. To The Student

This book is for those who either want to read some modern English poetry or have to read some for school, university, or exams. You don't need to have studied literature before. The aim of the book is to help you understand and enjoy English poetry, and so to give you tools and methods for appreciating the poetry you read in the future.

You can use the book with or without a teacher. If you are studying alone, you will need to check your answers in the Key at the end of the book. Since the study of literature sometimes requires a purely personal response, however, not all the exercises have a single correct answer. In these cases it would be useful to discuss your ideas with a teacher or friend.

The books in this series adopt a double approach: literary and linguistic. Each chapter contains a section of Language Practice which is always based on the literature, and in almost all cases leads back into it. The result is that the two approaches 'feed' each other: the linguistic study helping you appreciate the literature, and the literature helping you appreciate (and use) the language.

If you look now at the Contents page, you will see that most of the chapters in this book are organized around a topic: Childhood, Age, Love, and so on. Two chapters (Images and Satire) are organised slightly differently (around literary rather than general topics), but still follow the basic pattern of studying two or more related poems in comparison with each other.

You can work on the chapters in any order you like, but we suggest that you begin at least with Chapters 1 to 3. This is because Chapter 1, Childhood, deals with a topic on which we are all, by definition, well qualified to hold an opinion. Chapter 2, Age, provides an introduction to the important technical business of metre and rhyme, while Chapter 3, Images, deals with the equally important business of metaphors, similes and symbols. Once you have grasped these ideas, and are happy with them, you can work through the rest of the book in your own way.

Finally, in order to make the best of this book, you should (indeed *must*) have (1) a good monolingual English dictionary, (2) a good bilingual dictionary, and (3) a handbook of English grammar and usage. You may also (4) want to know more about the historical and cultural background to the poems you read here. The following is a basic list of suggestions to cover these needs:

(1) *Oxford Advanced Learner's Dictionary* or *Longman Dictionary of Contemporary English.*

(2) This will depend on what is available, but buy a large, modern dictionary if possible. Ask the advice of someone who knows both languages well. A good dictionary is a marvellous intellectual tool which will serve you for many years. It should (a) translate a large number of words, (b) give all the possible meanings for these words, and (c) reflect past as well as modern usage. Avoid mini-dictionaries, therefore, which have their place in the tourist's suitcase but are useless for the study of literature.

(3) Jake Allsop, *Cassell's Students' English Grammar* (Cassell)
A J Thomson & A V Martinet, *A Practical English Grammar* (Oxford)
Raymond Murphy, *English Grammar In Use* (Cambridge)
Michael Swan, *Practical English Usage* (Oxford)

(4) Harry Blamires, *Twentieth Century English Literature* (Macmillan)
John Press, *A Map of Modern English Verse* (Oxford)
Boris Ford (editor), *The Pelican Guide to English Literature*, Volumes 7 and 8 (Penguin)

2. To The Teacher

Little needs to be added except to note that, although the book is written with private study in mind, practically every exercise in the book will work in the classroom with little or no adaptation. Some exercises, in fact, are specifically designed for groupwork already (see for example Chapter 1, Question 2).

As the use of literature in the language class is still something of a novelty (albeit a rediscovered one), it's worth pointing out to the wary that the application of communicative teaching techniques to the study of literature can, with a bit of imagination and flexibility, produce excellent results. Time spent on thinking up suitable ways to introduce games, dramatization, surveys, quizzes, puzzles, debates, role-plays, projects, etc – all of which enhance student motivation – will usually pay very handsome returns. But in setting up any group activity (especially a discussion) it is essential to give the student a specific goal – a decision to be reached – in a specific time. The vague, leaden approach of 'discuss Question Four', followed inevitably by 'discuss Question Five', is not likely to be much of a success in any context.

One more suggestion. With poetry in particular, some practice in reading aloud is essential. This may seem old-fashioned, and against the prevailing theoretical orthodoxy, but poetry is at least as much a musical as a verbal art, and it just cannot be appreciated unless it is spoken, aloud, by the student. Again, a little ingenuity and enthusiasm can turn this activity into something enjoyable and illuminating. To overcome inhibitions, group recitation can be effective, particularly if conducted with zest and in small, surprise doses. To get some expression into the students' reading, you can try imposing interpretations: 'read this as if you think it's the most wonderful poem in the world', 'read this as if you're in love with the person you're reading to', 'read this as a politician might read it', and so on. This very mild form of role-playing often liberates the imagination in quite surprising ways, and leads naturally into questions of literary interpretation too.

Finally, if you find yourself disagreeing violently with the answers in the Key, you can of course treat them as further discussion points. It is probably unwise to suggest that *all* the literary questions are debatable, since this can open the door to the worst kinds of crackpot theorizing and the false idea that everything is subjective. However, a good many of the questions certainly are debatable, at least to the extent that there is more to be said. Students should be encouraged to recognise this as part of their developing critical approach.

Alex Martin
Robert Hill

1 Childhood

Sark Girl by Guy Malet
(Victoria and Albert Museum)

Before you read

1   What are your earliest memories? Are they of people? Of toys? Of things you did? Of things you saw others doing? Are they happy, sad, neutral? Write down three of them in as much detail as you can.

2   Group activity. Draw a picture (no matter how crude) of an important scene from your childhood. Show it to another member of the group, and answer his/her questions about it. When you've answered all the questions, look at your partner's picture and ask questions about that.

3   Read the following poems. As you read, say which of the poems is written from the following points of view:
    a)   a man thinking about a child
    b)   a child
    c)   a man looking back to his own childhood

Children's Song

We live in our own world,
A world that is too small
For you to stoop and enter
Even on hands and knees,
5   The adult subterfuge.
And though you probe and pry
With analytic eye,
And eavesdrop all our talk
With an amused look,
10   You cannot find the centre
Where we dance, where we play,
Where life is still asleep
Under the closed flower,
Under the smooth shell
15   Of eggs in the cupped nest
That mock the faded blue
Of your remoter heaven.

R S Thomas

Vocabulary
stoop: *bend down*
subterfuge: *trick*
probe: *investigate*
pry: *secretly look*
eavesdrop: *secretly listen*
cupped: *in the shape of a cup*

Dead Dog

One day I found a lost dog in the street.
The hairs about its grin were spiked with blood,
And it lay still as stone. It must have been
A little dog, for though I only stood
5   Nine inches for each one of my four years
I picked it up and took it home. My mother
Squealed, and later father spaded out
A bed and tucked my mongrel down in mud.

I can't remember any feeling but
10   A moderate pity, cool not swollen-eyed;
Almost a godlike feeling now it seems.
My lump of dog was ordinary as bread.
I have no recollection of the school
Where I was taught my terror of the dead.

Vernon Scannell

> **Vocabulary**
> grin: *big happy smile*
> spiked with blood: *with drops of blood on the ends*
> nine inches . . . four years: *his height was 36 inches (91 cm)*
> squealed: *gave a cry of fright*
> spaded out: *dug with a spade*
> tucked: *put into bed*
> mongrel: *dog of mixed breed*
> swollen-eyed: *with eyes swollen from tears*
> godlike: *like a god, superhuman*
> lump: *shapeless piece*
> recollection: *memory*

Incendiary

That one small boy with a face like pallid cheese
And burnt-out little eyes could make a blaze
As brazen, fierce and huge, as red and gold
And zany yellow as the one that spoiled
5   Three thousand guineas' worth of property
And crops at Godwin's Farm on Saturday
Is frightening – as fact and metaphor:
An ordinary match intended for
The lighting of a pipe or kitchen fire
10   Misused may set a whole menagerie
Of flame-fanged tigers roaring hungrily.
And frightening, too, that one small boy should set
The sky on fire and choke the stars to heat
Such skinny limbs and such a little heart
15   Which would have been content with one warm kiss
Had there been anyone to offer this.

Vernon Scannell

> **Vocabulary**
> incendiary: *one who deliberately starts a destructive fire*
> pallid: *pale*
> blaze: *vigorous fire*
> brazen: *shameless (literally, made of brass)*
> zany: *playful*
> guinea: *old unit of money worth £1.05*
> menagerie: *zoo*
> flame-fanged: *with teeth of fire*
> choke: *prevent from breathing, suffocate*
> skinny: *very thin*
> content: *happy*
> had there been: *if there had been*

First reaction

4   Compare the poems to the following quotations. Do you see any connections?

a)   'Don't be afraid to love him and enjoy him. Every baby needs to be smiled at, talked to, played with, fondled –

gently and lovingly – just as much as he needs vitamins and calories. That's what will make him a person who loves people and enjoys life. The baby who doesn't get any loving will grow up cold and unresponsive.'

Dr Benjamin Spock, *Baby and Child Care*

b) 'Let us then suppose the mind to be, as we say, white paper, void of all characters, without any ideas: How comes it to be furnished? Whence comes it by that vast store which the busy and boundless fancy of man has painted on it with an almost endless variety? Whence has it all the materials of reason and knowledge? To this I answer, in one word, from EXPERIENCE.'

John Locke

c) 'We know nothing of childhood: and with our mistaken notions the further we advance the further we go astray. The wisest writers devote themselves to what a man ought to know, without asking what a child is capable of learning. They are always looking for the man in the child, without considering what he is before he becomes a man.'

Jean-Jacques Rousseau, Preface to *Emile*

d) 'Let us lay it down as an incontrovertible rule that the first impulses of nature are always right; there is no original sin in the human heart; the how and why of the entrance of every vice can be traced.'

Jean-Jacques Rousseau, Preface to *Emile*

e) 'Children's games are not games: they must be considered as their most serious actions.'

Michel de Montaigne, *Essays*

f) 'It is before they get to school that children are likely to do their best learning . . . Children have a style of learning that fits their condition, and which they use naturally and well until we train them out of it.'

John Holt, *How Children Learn*

Close reading

5   Look again at these lines from 'Children's Song'.

. . . eggs in the cupped nest
That mock the faded blue
Of your remoter heaven.

The word 'mock' means to mimic or ridicule. The word 'heaven' means sky or paradise. It's easy to see how birds' eggs, being blue, mimic the sky; but how can they ridicule the sky, or the paradise, of adults? And why is the adult heaven 'faded blue' and 'remoter'?

6   I have no recollection of the school
Where I was taught my terror of the dead.

Say whether the following statements are true or false:

a) He found the dead dog near the school, but he can't remember where the school was.
b) He can't remember where he learnt his terror of the dead.
c) School was much less memorable for him than finding a dead dog.
d) Finding the dog taught him to fear death.
e) He thinks that children are not naturally afraid of death.
f) He was already a schoolboy when he found the dog.
g) He no longer fears death.
h) He has never feared death.

7   Look again at 'Incendiary' and answer the questions.

a)   . . . one small boy with a face like pallid cheese
And burnt-out little eyes . . .

What do these words suggest about the boy? (Is he healthy? happy? well cared for? communicative?)

b)   . . . a blaze
As brazen, fierce and huge, as red and gold
And zany yellow . . .

The contrast between the fire and the boy is striking. Does this tell us any more about the boy? Which of the two – the fire or the boy – seems more alive?

c) The contrast between something small, apparently insignificant, and its huge destructive potential, is repeated later on in the poem – twice. Can you see where?

d)   . . . to heat
Such skinny limbs and such a little heart

Whose limbs and heart are these?

e) Pick out all the words in the poem that refer to fire or heat.

f) What kind of warmth is the poet referring to in the phrase 'warm kiss'? Is it physical or emotional warmth? Is this the same as, or different from, the warmth suggested by the other words referring to fire and heat in the poem?

Language practice – structures

8 It must have been a little dog, for . . . I picked it up and took it home.

This is how we express a deduction about the past. We could also express this sentence as follows:

I picked it up and took it home, so it must have been a little dog.

Complete the following sentences, using *must have* . . .

a) The boy's mother squealed, so she _____ afraid.

b) The dog lay still in the street, so it _____ dead.

c) The boy who started the fire is described in detail, so the poet _____

d) There were crops at Godwin's farm, so _____ summer or autumn.

e) A lot of crops and property were damaged, so the fire _____

9 For a negative deduction about the past we use *can't have* or *couldn't have*.

Example: *I carried the dog home, so it can't have been very big.*

Now complete these sentences using *can't have*:

a) The boy learned terror of the dead at school, so he _____

b) He says his pity was 'moderate', so he _____

c) He has no recollection of school, so it _____

d) The boy had no-one to kiss him, so _____

e) 'Guineas' became obsolete in 1976, so the events of the poem _____

10

Though you probe and pry . . . you cannot find the centre.

Though I only stood three feet tall I picked it up.

a) How would you re-write these sentences using *but* or *yet*?

b) Re-write the following sentences using *though* or *although* (Note: *although* is slightly more formal than *though*, but otherwise they are interchangeable):

Adults crawl on hands and knees, yet they cannot enter the child's world.
Adults have a heaven, but it is faded and remote.
Adults listen to children, yet they can never understand them completely.
The boy called the dog 'my mongrel', but he did not own it.

The boy did not cry about the dog, but he still felt pity.
The boy's father knew it wasn't his son's dog, but he still buried it for him.
The dog is said to have a 'grin', yet it can't have been happy.

c)   Now complete these sentences using *though* or *although*:

'Incendiary'

_____, he managed to start an enormous fire.

_____, they can also be used to cause destruction.

_____, the poet sees him as a victim of neglect.

'Children's Song'

_____, the poet writes as if he were a child.

_____, he seems to enter it quite successfully.

_____, it is also a celebration of childhood.

d)   Re-write your sentences in c), using *yet*.

Vocabulary

11 Fill in the missing words in this passage:

English vocabulary is more or less equally _____ (1) of words from two largely separate _____ (2) traditions: Germanic (derived from Old English _____ (3) Scandinavian) and Romance (derived from French and Latin). The Germanic _____ (4) is longer established in Britain, having entered in the fifth century A.D. Its _____ (5) are usually shorter than those of Romance origin, and _____ (6) given modern English its names for much of the physical _____ (7) (weather, animals, houses, settlements and so on), _____ (8) key concepts and emotions, as _____ (9) as its numbers, pronouns, and conjunctions. The Romance tradition _____ (10) with the Norman invasion of 1066, when French _____ (11) established as the language of the court, of politics and administration. Words from Norman French _____ (12) to be polysyllabic, as well as _____ (13) technical, intellectual, or abstract. Gradually, the two traditions _____ (14), and an English language that is a

_____ (15) ancestor of today's was being _____ (16) and written in England by about 1400.

This double tradition makes _____ (17) a language unusually rich in synonyms. You will often _____ (18) that there are at least two words _____ (19) the same object or idea, with one or more coming from _____ (20) tradition. Here are some examples:

Germanic	Romance
fire	conflagration
dog-like	canine
live	exist
crops	produce
small	diminutive
friendly	amicable
godlike	divine

The polysyllabic or Latin-derived word is often _____ (21) as more 'educated', 'difficult' or 'official'. The _____ (22) Germanic words are thought of as _____ (23) 'common' and 'instinctive', more expressive of true feeling. The language _____ (24) scholarship, politics and bureaucracy is therefore, _____ (25) you might expect, filled with Latin-derived words. However, the _____ (26) vivid and forceful uses of the _____ (27) almost always contain a high proportion of Germanic vocabulary.

12 Using the information from Question 11 as a guide, go through the poem 'Dead Dog' and count the words that you think come from each of the two main roots of English (Germanic and Romance)
   a) in lines 1–8
   b) in lines 9–14

13 You should find a considerable difference between the two parts of the poem. Can you think of a reason for this?

Extension

14 In 1794, the poet William Blake (1757-1827) published a poem
called 'The School Boy', which begins like this:

I love to rise in a summer morn,
When the birds sing on every tree;
The distant huntsman winds his horn,
And the sky-lark sings with me.
O! what sweet company.

But to go to school in a summer morn,
O! it drives all joy away;
Under a cruel eye outworn,
The little ones spend the day,
In sighing and dismay.

William Blake

> **Vocabulary**
> morn: *morning*
> winds: *blows*
> outworn: *worn out,*
>   *lifeless*
> dismay: *unhappiness*

Is this how you remember your schooldays, or were they
happier?

Do you think these lines from the poem are still true for children
today?

Beyond the text

15 Here are some English nursery rhymes (traditional songs and
poems for children). What is it that appeals to children in these
poems?

There was a crooked man,
And he walked a crooked mile,
He found a crooked sixpence
Beside a crooked stile,
He bought a crooked cat,
Which caught a crooked mouse,
And they all lived together
In a crooked little house.

*   *   *

Baa, baa, black sheep, have you any wool?
Yes, sir, yes, sir, three bags full.
One for the master, one for the dame,
And one for the little boy who lives down the lane.

> **Vocabulary**
> crooked: *opposite of*
>   *straight*
> dame: *woman*
> fiddle: *violin*
> sport: *fun*

Hey Diddle Diddle
by Mark Martin

Hey diddle diddle, the cat and the fiddle,
The cow jumped over the moon.
The little dog laughed to see such sport
And the dish ran away with the spoon.

* * *

Wee Willie Winkie runs through the town,
Upstairs and downstairs in his night gown,
Rapping at the windows, crying through the lock,
'Are the children all in bed, for it's past eight o'clock?'

Wee Willie Winkie
by William Martin

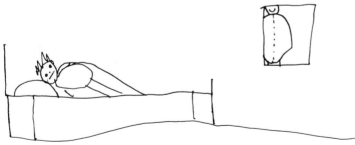

16 What nursery rhymes do you remember? Are there any similarities between them and the English ones quoted above?

17 Group activity. Teach one of the nursery rhymes you remember to another person in the group. Explain its meaning as far as possible.

Authors

R S Thomas was born in Cardiff in 1913 and studied Classics at the University of Wales. He was a priest in the Church of Wales from 1937 until his retirement in 1978. His poetry is much influenced by his experience as a country clergyman in remote and economically depressed parts of Wales, and much of it concerns his own struggle to see the operation of God's grace in these bleak, harsh surroundings. He has published several volumes of poems over 45 years, including *Selected Poems 1946-68* (1973). His latest book is *Counterpoint* (Bloodaxe Books, 1990). He received the Queen's Gold Medal for Poetry in 1964.

Vernon Scannell was born in 1922 in Lincolnshire. He served in the Gordon Highlanders during World War II, an experience which he was later to turn memorably into poetry. He studied at Leeds University, then worked as a professional boxer, and later as a schoolteacher. Since 1962 he has been a full-time writer and broadcaster. He has published several novels, children's books, anthologies of poetry, an autobiography (*The Tiger and the Rose*, 1971) and *New and Collected Poems 1950-80*. He has said of his own work, 'Major themes: violence, the experience of war, the "sense of danger" which is part of the climate of our times; these are contrasted with poems of a more private nature which affirm the continuity and indestructibility of the creative spirit.'

2 Age

*Pearly King and Queen
(Hulton-Deutsch Collection)*

Before you read

1   Look at the photograph above. Why do you think these people
    are wearing clothes decorated with hundreds of pearl buttons?
    How would you describe the expressions on their faces?

2   Write down ten things you know about old people.
    Eg *They forget easily.*

3   Are you worried by the thought of growing old? Is there anything
    you look forward to in old age?

    Read the poem on the next page.

Warning

When I am an old woman I shall wear purple
With a red hat which doesn't go, and doesn't suit me.
And I shall spend my pension on brandy and summer
    gloves
5 And satin sandals, and say we've no money for butter.
I shall sit down on the pavement when I'm tired
And gobble up samples in shops and press alarm bells
And run my stick along the public railings
And make up for the sobriety of my youth.
10 I shall go out in my slippers in the rain
And pick the flowers in other people's gardens
And learn to spit.

You can wear terrible shirts and grow more fat
And eat three pounds of sausages at a go
15 Or only bread and pickle for a week
And hoard pens and pencils and beermats and things
    in boxes.

But now we must have clothes that keep us dry
And pay our rent and not swear in the street
20 And set a good example for the children.
We must have friends to dinner and read the papers.

But maybe I ought to practise a little now?
So people who know me are not too shocked and
    surprised
25 When suddenly I am old, and start to wear purple.

Jenny Joseph

Vocabulary
doesn't go: *looks wrong
with the other colours*
doesn't suit me: *looks
wrong on me*
pension: *old person's
payments from the state*
gobble: *eat greedily*
make up: *compensate*
sobriety: *noun formed from
sober*
slippers: *soft shoes usually
worn indoors*
terrible: *ugly*
pound: *English/US measure
of weight (454 grams)*
at a go: *without stopping*
pickle: *vegetables preserved
in vinegar*
hoard: *collect*
beermat: *piece of card placed
under a beer glass*
swear: *use offensive or
obscene language*
papers: *newspapers*

First reaction

4   Complete this sentence using fewer than five words:

'Warning' is not just a poem about old age; it is also about

_____

Close reading

5   'Warning' is divided into four short sections, each with a different
topic.

Write down the topic of each section:

Lines	Topic
1-12	_____
13-17	_____
18-21	_____
22-25	_____

6   The way in which a poem's argument develops over its different sections is called its *structure*. In this poem, the four-part structure is made clearer by visual emphasis – gaps on the page where the new sections begin – also by grammatical emphasis. Look at the main verbs in the first section. They are all governed by the auxiliary *shall* with the pronoun *I*. Can you find a similar pattern in sections 2 and 3? Fill in the table.

Section	Auxiliary	Pronoun
1	_____	_____
2	_____	_____
3	_____	_____

7   Who is 'you' in line 13?
   a) her husband
   b) a female friend
   c) a male friend
   d) the reader
   e) people in general

8   Look at line 22: 'But maybe I ought to practise a little now?' Practise *what* precisely?

9   Of the following sentences choose the one which you think is closest in meaning to line 22:
   a) I must practise a little now.
   b) I would like to practise a little now.
   c) I think it would be sensible to practise a little now.
   d) Do you think I should practise a little now?

Language practice – vocabulary

10 Match the phrases A-L with the adjectives in 1-12

A	I shall wear purple	**1**	greedy
B	I shall spend my pension on brandy and summer gloves	**2**	scatter-brained
		3	mischievous
C	I shall sit down on the pavement when I'm tired	**4**	extravagant
D	. . . and press alarm bells	**5**	hospitable
E	. . . and run my stick along the public railings	**6**	well-behaved
F	. . . go out in my slippers in the rain	**7**	anti-social
G	. . . and pick the flowers in other people's gardens	**8**	responsible
H	. . . and learn to spit	**9**	offensive
I	. . . You can eat three pounds of sausages at a go	**10**	inconsiderate
J	. . . We must not swear in the street	**11**	garish
K	. . . and set a good example for the children	**12**	impulsive
L	. . . We must have friends to dinner		

A ____ B ____ C ____ D ____ E ____ F ____

G ____ H ____ I ____ J ____ K ____ L ____

11 Group Activity. Think of other examples of behaviour which are mischievous, scatter-brained, inconsiderate, etc. Then read out your examples, and your partner (or the rest of the group) must try to guess which adjective you are thinking of.

12 Write a short (one sentence) summary of each of the first three sections, using adjectives instead of verbs.

Example: Section 1 – *When she is old she would like to be mischievous, greedy and loud.*

Extension

13 Write a few lines of your own fantasy, beginning 'When I am old . . .'

14 The next poem begins, 'Death is the twin of Sleep, they say'. What similarities are there between death and sleep? What are the differences?

15 Now read this poem. Does it mention any similarities or differences that you didn't think of?

Off Wall Street by Jonathan Eastland

The Twin of Sleep

Death is the twin of Sleep, they say:
    For I shall rise renewed,
Free from the cramps of yesterday,
    Clear-eyed and supple-thewed.

5 But though this bland analogy
    Helps other folk to face
Decrepitude, senility,
    Madness, disease, disgrace,

I do not like Death's greedy looks:
10   Give me his twin instead –
Sleep never auctions off my books,
    My boots, my shirts, my bed.

Robert Graves

Vocabulary
cramps: *pains in the muscles*
supple-thewed: *with muscles*
 in good condition
bland: *simple, unexciting*
folk: *people*
face: *accept*
decrepitude: *extreme weakness*
 of old age
looks: *appearance*
auctions off: *sells (at auction)*

16 What difference do you notice immediately between this poem
and the poem 'Warning'?

17 a) Look at lines 2-4 of 'The Twin of Sleep'. Who says these things? Is it 'I' or 'they'?
  b) What does 'yesterday' mean in this context?
  c) According to the last verse, what is the difference between sleep and death? Put it in your own words.

18 a) Read the first line of this poem aloud (or listen to it being read by someone else), and mark the stressed syllables. How many are there?
  b) Do the same for the second line. How many?
  c) Repeat for lines 3 and 4.
  d) Do you see the same pattern repeated in the next eight lines?

Check your answers in the Key before going on.

19 The alternation of stressed and unstressed syllables is called *rhythm*. If there is a regular rhythm, it is called a *metre*, and a poem written with a metre is *metrical*. Poems without a metre are said to be written in *free verse*.

Now look at the first four lines of 'Warning' and mark the stressed syllables. Do you find a regular rhythm there? Now check another four lines (you choose which): are they metrical, or free verse?

20 There is another regularly-repeated element in 'The Twin of Sleep'. The last syllable of line 1 (*say*) makes the same sound as the last syllable of line 3 (*day*). This is called a *rhyme*. You will also see that the end of line 2 rhymes with the end of line 4. This pattern is repeated throughout the poem. When a rhyme pattern is repeated like this, it is called a *rhyme-scheme*, and each rhyme is given a letter, like this:
  line 1 (*say*) – a
  line 2 (-*newed*) – b
  line 3 (-*day*) – a
  line 4 (-*thewed*) – b

The rhyme-scheme of this poem is therefore said to be *a-b-a-b*. Labelling rhyme-schemes in this way usually does not tell you very much about a poem by itself, but it can be useful when comparing poems.

21 Do you think the metre and rhyme in 'The Twin of Sleep' add anything to the poem?

Language practice – structures

22 Both poems take a common idea and challenge it. We could say, for example, the following about 'The Twin of Sleep':

The poem challenges the common idea of death as a kind of sleep.

or *The poem challenges the common idea that death is a kind of sleep.*

Can you write two similar sentences about 'Warning'?

23 As well as challenging common ideas, poems can also remind us of important truths that we often forget. For example, when we think of old people, we often think only of negative things – physical weakness, the approach of death, and so on. We forget that old people are almost always interesting to talk to, individual (even eccentric) in their thoughts and habits, and free from the responsibilities and conventions that dominate the lives of younger people. We could therefore say, about the poem 'Warning', for example,

It reminds us that old age can liberate people. or
It reminds us of the liberation that can come with old age.

Now write two similar sentences about 'The Twin of Sleep':

It reminds us that _____

It reminds us of _____

24 Read the following poems in this book, and say how they challenge common ideas or remind us of important truths.
  a) Louis Simpson, 'Hubert's Museum' (page 83)
  b) D. H. Lawrence, 'Money-Madness' (pages 103-4)

Beyond the text

25 Detective work.
  On the next page is a poem with some of the words missing. Using only the clues given, see if you can fill the gaps. (If you get stuck, the full poem is printed in the Key.)

  Clues
  1 The poem's rhyme scheme is printed down the right hand side.
  2 All the missing words have just one syllable, except the word in line 12, which has two syllables.

Sonnet for the Class of '58

Rhyme-scheme

No longer students and not likely to succeed,	a
tonight I remember old friends, scattered far,	b
who wanted so much once, and now	a
only a rise of a hundred pounds or a .... ,	b
or a holiday abroad without the .... ,	c
or time to read more, or more fun.	d
Perhaps never, or only when drunk, does life	c
seem as it once seemed, a war to be	d
The moving and influential things they devised	e
have all been said and done, it seems, by others.	f
Some do the very things that they despised	e
and recognise the enemy as ....;	f
and even those who've gained more power or	g
feel sorry when they feel the difference.	g

Lines 5 and 10 are numbered in the margin.

Vocabulary
scattered far: *in many different places*
rise: *increase in salary*
moving: *impressive or beautiful*
influential: *having an influence on others*
the very things: *precisely those things*

James Simmons

26 **a)** 'who wanted so much once' (line 3) – what kinds of things do you think they wanted? Give some examples.
   b) 'the very things that they despised' (line 11) – what kinds of things are these? Can you think of some examples?
   c) 'the difference' (line 14) – what difference is this?

27 Essay or discussion topics:
   a) Is 'Sonnet for the Class of '58' optimistic or pessimistic about age?
   b) How would you describe the mood of each of the three poems in this chapter?
   c) Which of the three poems in this chapter most suits your feelings about age?
   d) Is there anything important about age which these poems fail to say?

Authors

Jenny Joseph was born in 1932 in Birmingham. She has published five volumes of verse, including *Selected Poems* (1989), and a novel, *Persephone*, written partly in poetry and partly in prose, which won the James Tait Black Memorial Prize in 1987. She lives in London.

Robert Graves (1895-1985) was born in London, and fought in France in the First World War straight after school. He was seriously wounded, but survived. After the war he studied at Oxford, then taught in Egypt. His life up to this point is recounted in one of the masterpieces of 20th century autobiography, *Goodbye To All That* (1929). Later he moved permanently to Majorca. Although he saw himself primarily as a poet, Graves also wrote a number of highly successful historical novels, of which *I, Claudius* (1934) is the best-known. He also wrote an entertaining and unusual guide to *The Greek Myths*, and a work on the sources of poetry, *The White Goddess*.

James Simmons was born in Londonderry in 1933, and studied at Leeds University. He has taught in Ireland and Nigeria, and now lives in Belfast. He is a singer and songwriter as well as a poet. He founded *The Honest Ulsterman*, Ireland's leading literary magazine, and the Poor Genius record company. He has received several major prizes for his poetry. His *Poems 1956-86* contains work from nine previous volumes.

3 Images

Wood Engraving by
Robert Gibbings
(The Bodleian Library)

Before you read

Look at the picture of a seagull above and compare it to the one on
the next page.

1   In particular, look at the following details of the first picture:
    –   the position of the wings
    –   the cloud shapes in the sky
    –   the eggs
    –   the position of the nest on a rock above the sea.

Herring Gull
by Taurus Graphics

a) What do they suggest to you about the bird?
b) Do you find any such suggestions in the second picture?

2   Do you think the artists who made these pictures had the same intentions? What do you think their intentions were?

3   Read the poems and the encyclopedia article that follows. What kinds of information do we find in
a) the poems
b) the article?

Autumn

A touch of cold in the Autumn night –
   I walked abroad
And saw the ruddy moon lean over a hedge
Like a red-faced farmer.
I did not stop to speak, but nodded,
And round about were the wistful stars
With white faces like town children.

T E Hulme

Above the Dock

Above the quiet dock in mid night,
   Tangled in the tall mast's corded height,
Hangs the moon. What seemed so far away
Is but a child's balloon, forgotten after play.

T E Hulme

London (May 1915) extract

At night, the moon, a pregnant woman,
Walks cautiously over the slippery heavens . . .

Richard Aldington

Moon, the /muːn/ the natural satellite of the Earth, 3,476 km/2,160 mi in diameter, with a mass ⅛₁ that of the Earth. Its average distance from Earth is 384,400 km/238,850 mi, and it orbits Earth every 27.32 days (the *sidereal month*). The Moon spins on its axis so that it keeps one side permanently turned towards the Earth. The Moon is illuminated by sunlight, and goes through a cycle of phases from New (invisible) via First Quarter (half Moon) to Full and back again to New, every 29.53 days (the *synodic month* also known as a **lunation**.)

The Moon has no air or water. On its sunlit side temperatures reach 110°C, but during the two-week lunar night the surface temperature drops to −170°C. Its composition is rocky, with a surface heavily scarred by meteorite impacts that have formed craters up to 240 km/150 mi across. The youngest craters are surrounded by bright rays of ejected rock. The largest scars have been filled in by dark lava to produce the lowland plains known as seas or *maria* (see mare). These dark patches form the familiar 'man-in-the-Moon' pattern. Rocks brought back by Apollo astronauts show the Moon is 4,600 million years old, the same age as the Earth. Unlike the Earth, most of the Moon's surface features were formed within the first 1,000 million years of its history when it was subjected to heavy bombardment by meteorites.

The origin of the Moon is open to debate. Theories suggest that it split from the Earth; that it was a separate body captured by Earth's gravity; or that it formed in orbit around the Earth. The latest idea suggests that the Moon was formed from debris thrown off when a body the size of Mars struck the Earth early in the Earth's history.

(Entry for 'Moon' from *Hutchinson Encyclopedia*)

---

4   Are there any parallels between the pictures of the gulls and the writings about the moon quoted above?

5   What is the object described in the following paragraph?

This object can be used either when working or relaxing. It is pale brown, almost a metre high, half a metre wide, and half a metre deep. It is made of wood. It is hard and smooth. In profile its shape is similar to the letter 'h'. It stands on four legs. It does not contain anything, but people or things are often placed on it. It is silent when it is used, but makes a loud scraping when pulled across the floor. It is decorated with two or three rings cut into the wood of its legs. It is not particularly expensive, yet solid and handsomely made. It was made in England about three years ago. It looks used, and is shiny in places where hands and clothes have rubbed it. There are marks and scratches on most of its surfaces.

6   Now it's your turn. Take an object that you can see, or have often seen, and describe it in two ways:
   a)   like a short article for an encyclopaedia, giving basic facts such as size, shape, colour, etc.
   b)   like one of the poems by Hulme and Aldington.

7   Compare the description you have written in a) with the description you have written in b). Which one gives you the clearer picture in your mind? Which do you find more interesting?

In Question 6 a) you used only facts about the object to describe it. In 6 b) you used images. The use of images is one of the fundamental techniques of writing, especially poetry. We also use them frequently in speech, in phrases like 'he eats like a pig' or 'she's like a breath of fresh air'. They provide a picture or idea of the object through similarities, helping the reader or listener to imagine it for himself.

There are many different kinds of image, but we will look at four different types here:
Simile (pronounced **'sɪmɪlɪ**)
Metaphor (pronounced **'metəfə(r)**)
Symbol
Narrative or descriptive images

Simile

Definition: a simile is an explicit comparison between the object A and another object B, in the form 'A is like B', or 'A is as . . . [adjective] as B'.
For a simile to work, there must be some similarity or point of comparison between A and B.

Example

> I walked abroad,
> And saw the ruddy moon lean over the hedge
> Like a red-faced farmer.

Object A is the moon. Object B is a red-faced farmer. The similarity or point of comparison is a red shape, which is familiar and reassuring, appearing over the hedge.

(NOTE: A and B do not necessarily have to be objects in the limited sense of 'inanimate physical things'. They can equally be people, animals, qualities, ideas, etc. We have used the word 'object' in this wider sense both here and in the following definitions.)

8   Now read the poem on the next page and answer the questions.

Fan-Piece, for her Imperial Lord

O fan of white silk,
    clear as frost on the grass-blade,
You also are laid aside.

Ezra Pound

a)   What is the object described by the poet?
b)   What is the simile used by the poet as a comparison?
c)   What is the point of comparison between them?

Metaphor

(adjective *metaphorical*; adverb *metaphorically*)

Definition: a metaphor is an implicit comparison between the object A and another object B. It takes the form 'A is B'. A metaphor is not always a noun. It can also be a verb, adjective or adverb. As with a simile, there must be some similarity or point of comparision between A and B.

Example

    Above the quiet dock in mid night,
        Tangled in the tall mast's corded height,
    Hangs the moon. What seemed so far away
    Is but a child's balloon, forgotten after play.
                                    T E Hulme

Object A is the moon. Object B is a child's balloon. The similarity or point of comparison is a round shape, with a cord leading to it; and something which was once perceived as magical but whose magic has gone.

9   Read this poem and answer the questions.

Fog

The fog comes
on little cat feet.

It sits looking
over harbor and city
on silent haunches
and then moves on.
                Carl Sandburg

Vocabulary
haunches: *upper part of the legs*

a)   What is the object described by the poet?
b)   What is the metaphor used by the poet as a comparison?
c)   What is the point of comparison between them?

Symbol

(adjective *symbolic*; adverb *symbolically*)

Definition: a symbol is the representation of an idea A by an Object B. The idea A is not mentioned at all, only suggested.

Examples

Symbol		*Idea*
Heart		Love
Dove		Peace
Sword		War
Poet writes: 'O fan of white silk'		Reader thinks: 'elegant woman'

10 Say what the following symbols usually represent (or could represent):
a)   a lion
b)   a mouse
c)   a snake
d)   a shield
e)   a hammer
f)   a field of wheat

11 Group activity. Write down, or draw, some symbols of your own. Include some which are not well known and have a purely private meaning. Show them to another member of the group, and ask them to guess what they stand for. What happens when you show them the private symbols? Is it possible to guess them? How?

Narrative or Descriptive images

Definition: a narrative or descriptive image occurs where the object A is presented on its own without comment, usually as part of a sequence or story; it is essentially a word-picture and nothing else. The reader is not expected to think of anything but the picture or object itself. (In this it is different from similes, metaphors and symbols.)

Example:

Image from D'Orléans

Young men riding in the street
In the bright new season
Spur without reason
Causing their steeds to leap.

And at the pace they keep
Their horses' armoured feet
Strike sparks from the cobbled street
In the bright new season.

Ezra Pound

> **Vocabulary**
> spur: *incite; dig their (spiked)*
>   *heels into the horses' sides*
> steed: *(archaic) horse*
> pace: *speed, rhythm*
> armoured: *with metal shoes*
> cobbled: *surface made of small*
>   *stones*

12 a)   What are the objects described by the poet?
   b)   What do you think is the poet's purpose in describing this scene?

Close Reading

Evening

The chimneys, rank on rank,
Cut the clear sky;
The moon
with a rag of gauze about her loins
Poses among them, an awkward Venus –

And here am I looking wantonly at her
Over the kitchen sink.

Richard Aldington

> **Vocabulary**
> rank on rank: *in multiple rows*
>   *('rank' usually means a row of*
>   *soldiers)*
> rag: *torn piece of cloth*
> gauze: *thin, transparent cotton*
> loins: *the part of the body where*
>   *the legs join; the genital region*
> poses: *stands or sits like an*
>   *artist's model*
> wantonly: *full of desire*

13 All the images listed below are of the same type:

> rank on rank
> cut the clear sky
> a rag of gauze about her loins
> poses among them
> an awkward Venus

   a) Which type of image are they?
   b) In each case, what is being compared to what? (What is object 'A? What is object B?)
   c) In each case, what is the point of comparison between A and B?

14 What type of image do we find in the last two lines of the poem?

15 What is the effect of the last line? Choose from the following:
   a) a slightly comical anticlimax
   b) a feeling of domestic happiness
   c) a feeling of imprisonment

16 Read this poem and answer the questions.

Thaw

Over the land freckled with snow half-thawed
The speculating rooks at their nests cawed
And saw from elm-tops, delicate as flower of grass,
What we below could not see, Winter pass.

Edward Thomas

> **Vocabulary**
> thaw: *the melting of ice or snow*
> freckled: *spotted*
> speculating: *thinking*
> elm: *tree of the genus Ulmus*

   a) There is one simile in the poem. What is it?
   b) What is Thomas trying to help us imagine with this simile? Is it the elm-tops or the passing of winter? Or both?
   c) What are the points of comparison between them?

17 Read this poem and answer the questions.

Tall Nettles

Tall nettles cover up, as they have done
These many springs, the rusty harrow, the plough
Long worn out, and the roller made of stone:
Only the elm butt tops the nettles now.

This corner of the farmyard I like most:
As well as any bloom upon a flower
I like the dust on nettles, never lost
Except to prove the sweetness of a shower.

Edward Thomas

Vocabulary
springs: *refers to the season*
harrow, plough, roller: *farm
  implements, drawn behind a
  horse or tractor;*
elm butt: *the stump of an elm
  tree*
tops: *stands above*
bloom: *fresh beauty*

a) What types of images are there in this poem?
b) What do you think is the poet's purpose in describing this scene?
c) Compare the way Aldington introduces a speaker 'I' into the poem 'Evening'. What similarities and what differences do you notice in the effect of the 'I' figure in the two poems?

18 Read this poem.

Preludes

I

The winter evening settles down
With smells of steaks in passageways.
Six o'clock.
The burnt-out ends of smoky days.
5   And now a gusty shower wraps
The grimy scraps
Of withered leaves about your feet
And newspapers from vacant lots;
The showers beat
10 On broken blinds and chimney-pots,
And at the corner of the street
A lonely cab-horse steams and stamps.

And then the lighting of the lamps.

Vocabulary
gusty: *with gusts of wind*
grimy: *dirty*
vacant lots: *unused pieces of
  land in a city*
blinds: *screens to cover windows*
chimney-pots: *the tops of
  chimneys*
cab-horse: *taxis were still horse-
  drawn at this date (c.1910)*

II
The morning comes to consciousness
15 Of faint stale smells of beer
From the sawdust-trampled street
With all its muddy feet that press
To early coffee-stands.

With the other masquerades
20 That time resumes,
One thinks of all the hands
That are raising dingy shades
In a thousand furnished rooms.

III
You tossed a blanket from the bed,
25 You lay upon your back, and waited:
You dozed, and watched the night revealing
The thousand sordid images
Of which your soul was constituted;
They flickered against the ceiling.
30 And when all the world came back
And the light crept up between the shutters
And you heard the sparrows in the gutters,
You had such a vision of the street
As the street hardly understands;
35 Sitting along the bed's edge, where
You curled the papers from your hair,
Or clasped the yellow soles of feet
In the palms of both soiled hands.

IV
His soul stretched tight across the skies
40 That fade behind a city block,
Or trampled by insistent feet
At four and five and six o'clock;
And short square fingers stuffing pipes,
And evening newspapers, and eyes
45 Assured of certain certainties,
The conscience of a blackened street
Impatient to assume the world.
I am moved by fancies that are curled
Around these images, and cling:
50 The notion of some infinitely gentle
Infinitely suffering thing.

Wipe your hand across your mouth, and laugh;
The worlds revolve like ancient women
Gathering fuel in vacant lots.

                                                T S Eliot

sawdust: *dust from cut wood, used for cleaning the floors of shops and bars, then swept out onto the pavement*
coffee-stands: *outdoor coffee bars*
masquerades: *literally, theatrical shows in which the actors wear masks; but used here metaphorically to mean the 'theatre' of everyday life*
resumes: *begins again*
dingy: *old, cheap and worn*
shades: *a form of blinds*
furnished rooms: *cheap rented rooms*

tossed: *threw*
dozed: *slept lightly, half asleep, half awake*
sordid: *dirty and unpleasant*
flickered: *rapidly alternated light and shade, like pictures on a cinema screen*
crept: *moved slowly and quietly*
sparrow: *small bird (Passer domesticus)*
gutters: *sides of the road, below the edge of the pavement*
papers: *used to curl women's hair*
soles: *bottom of the feet*
soiled: *dirty*

stuffing pipes: *filling pipes with tobacco*
fancies: *fantasies, imagined things*
cling: *hold on tight*
notion: *idea*

First reaction

19   What feelings about city life does this poem arouse in you:
cynicism – amusement – confusion – blankness – joy – curiosity
– excitement – pleasure – depression – anger – tenderness – pity?

Close reading

20 a)   Pick out the phrases that refer to times of day in the poem.
    b)   Do you notice any chronological structure in the poem?

21   burnt-out ends
    smoky days
    grimy scraps
    withered leaves . . .

    a)   Can you find some more examples of these adjective-noun pairs in the poem?
    b)   Do the adjectives have anything in common?
    c)   Why do you think there are so many plural nouns?
    d)   What is the feeling created by these images?

22   His soul stretched tight across the skies
    That fade behind a city block,
    Or trampled by insistent feet
    At four and five and six o'clock;

    Do you think this means
    a)   One particular neurotic man finds city life unbearable?
    b)   Human beings in general find city life unbearable?
    c)   The souls of suffering mankind are like a membrane across the sky, excluding man from God?
    d)   The tensions and humiliations of life in the city are so great that man's soul is in danger of destruction?
    e)   Every man is full of dreams and ambitions, but these are crushed and trampled by everyday routine?

    (Note: if you think that more than one of these explanations is possible, say which ones they are, and place them in order of preference.)

23   The word 'images' is used twice in the poem (at lines 27 and 49). Carefully read the sentences in which the word is used, then choose the definition of 'images' that fits Eliot's meaning most closely:
    1   An artificial imitation or representation of the external form of any object, especially of a person; a statue; a likeness, portrait or picture.

2   An optical appearance or counterpart of an object, such as is produced by rays of light either reflected as from a mirror, refracted as through a lens, or falling on a surface after passing through a small aperture.

3   Appearance, form, semblance.

4   A counterpart, or copy; a symbol, emblem, or representation.

5   A mental representation of something (especially a visible object); a mental picture or impression; an idea or conception.

6   A vivid or graphic description.

7   A simile, metaphor, or figure of speech.

(all from the *Oxford English Dictionary*, 1933)

24 There seem to be three individual characters in this poem, referred to only by the pronouns *your/you* (female, because of the curled hair-papers), *his*, and *I*. Who do you think these characters might be? Why don't they have names?

25 Which of these explanations of the last three lines do you prefer?

a) The 'ancient women gathering fuel' are symbols for our souls; 'the worlds' are our experiences, which 'revolve' or repeat every day; Eliot's meaning is clear: that life is a tedious obligatory task, desolate, comfortless, and with no other purpose than simply staying alive. The 'laugh' is therefore a nervous laugh, not a sign of gaiety but of deep anxiety. It's a very depressing end to a very depressing poem.

b) These lines are simply a distraction: a false cynical note placed at the end of the poem by an embarrassed Eliot, wishing to cover up the tenderness of 'some infinitely gentle infinitely suffering thing'. What Eliot really believed in was that tenderness, but he was afraid to say so directly.

c) These lines are part of a precise dialectical movement: the thesis is the romantic four lines beginning 'I am moved', the antithesis is these last three anti-romantic lines, and the synthesis is left to the reader to construct for himself. 'You choose,' says Eliot.

d) Eliot's conclusion is that the only answer to the problem of unavoidable suffering is to laugh. Life goes on ('the worlds revolve'), so why worry about it? One might as well try to be happy.

e) 'Dash it away, this absurd degrading suggestion that there is anything good to be discovered in these worlds of the town; laugh at it, it is as futile as the plight of the destitute old woman who must glean for fuel in derelict building-sites. There remains, though, in the very choice of this image the same ambiguity as the whole poem conveys. An old woman searching for fuel is more likely to arouse our pity for helplessness and loneliness than our scorn or derision.' T S Pearce, *T S Eliot* (London, 1967) p.84.

Extension

26 Which of the poems in this chapter do you like? Which do you dislike? Can you say why?

27 Write a short image-poem of your own.

Authors

T E Hulme (1883-1917) was an important figure in the London avant-garde of the years before the First World War, despite the fact that his 'Complete Poetical Works', as published in 1912, consisted of just five poems ... His theoretical writings were influential in the revolt against the decadent romanticism of the late 19th Century, and in favour of the 'hard dry image'. He was a friend of Ezra Pound, and a member of the Imagist group. He fought and died in World War I.

Richard Aldington (1892-1962) was also a friend of Pound and an Imagist. He fought in World War I, but survived to describe it in his novel *Death of a Hero* (1929). In 1928 he left England, and lived in France and the USA. He wrote several novels, controversial biographies of D H Lawrence and T E Lawrence, critical essays, and an autobiography, *Life for Life's Sake* (1941).

Edward Thomas (1878-1917). See question 17, page 74.

Ezra Pound (1885-1972). See page 53.

T S Eliot (1888-1965) was born in St Louis, Missouri, and studied at Harvard, the Sorbonne, and Oxford. He settled in London in 1914, worked for a short while as a schoolmaster, then for eight years (1917-25) at Lloyd's Bank before joining the publishing house of Faber and Faber. 'Preludes' was published in Eliot's first book, *Prufrock and other Observations* (1917). In 1922 he founded an influential new literary magazine, *The Criterion*, and published his masterpiece, *The Waste Land*. Eliot was one of the key figures (with

Pound and Joyce) in the Modernist movement, and he is justly credited with transforming the language of English poetry in a way that brilliantly and disturbingly reflects the spirit of this century. A good part of his skill as a poet lay in using and adapting techniques, phrases, ideas, images, even whole lines from other writers: he owed much to the French 19th Century poets Baudelaire and Laforgue, but also to Dante, Webster, Donne, Shakespeare and many others. He was one of the greatest literary critics of the century. His major works, which include the remarkable poetic sequence *Four Quartets* (1935-42) and some memorable essays, have provided a feast for scholars, and exercised an enormous influence on all subsequent writing in English (and many other languages too.) He won the Nobel Prize for Literature in 1948.

4 Woman

Viba by Gerald Brockhurst
(The Ashmolean Museum)

This chapter contains three poems about women, written by men. None of the poems is about love in the romantic sense, which is the subject of the next chapter. These poems deal with less obvious feelings, each in a different way.

Before you read

1   A famous British actor once said in an interview, 'The only thing I look for in a woman is beauty. Everything else can be bought or learned.'

Do you think he is right? If not, what would you say in reply?

2 What do most men look for in a woman? Put these in order of
   priority –

   kindness   _____
   beauty   _____
   sense of humour   _____
   good taste   _____
   youth   _____
   intelligence   _____
   wit   _____
   cheerfulness   _____
   elegance   _____
   career prospects   _____

3 Read this poem and fill in the table below it.

Sindhi Woman

Barefoot through the bazaar,
and with the same undulant grace
as the cloth blown back from her face,
she glides with a stone jar
5 high on her head
and not a ripple in her tread.

Watching her cross erect
stones, garbage, excrement, and crumbs
of glass in the Karachi slums,
10 I, with my stoop, reflect
they stand most straight
who learn to walk beneath a weight.

Jon Stallworthy

> **Vocabulary**
> Sindhi: *from the region of Sind (Pakistan)*
> barefoot: *with bare feet*
> undulant: *moving like waves in the sea*
> glides: *moves slowly and smoothly*
> ripple: *small wave*
> tread: *step*
> erect: *with upright posture*
> slums: *poor, squalid part of the city*
> stoop: *opposite of erect*
> reflect: *think*

Topic	Write here what the poet says about it
The woman's clothes	
Her economic status	
Her movements	
Karachi	
Himself	

Close reading

4 Which of the topics mentioned in the table above does the poet stress most?

5 Look back at your answers to Questions 1 and 2. Is there anything you would like to know about this woman which the poet does not tell us?

6 **a)** The poet tells us the woman is from Sind. Where do you think *he* is from? Choose the answer from this list:
   – Karachi
   – Sind
   – somewhere else in Pakistan
   – some other country
b) Can you find anything in the poem to support your opinion?

7 What is the 'weight' in the last line? Does it have a secondary or symbolic meaning? If so, what?

8 The poem ends with a 'moral' – that is, an epigram expressing a philosophical or ethical idea. Explain in your own words what this 'moral' is.

9 **a)** Do you think this moral is generally true?
   b) Can you think of an example which might prove the opposite of this moral?
   c) Write the opposite moral.

10 Read this poem.

Liu Ch'e

The rustling of the silk is discontinued,
Dust drifts over the courtyard,
There is no sound of foot-fall, and the leaves
Scurry into heaps and lie still,
And she the rejoicer of the heart is beneath them:

A wet leaf that clings to the threshold.

Ezra Pound

> **Vocabulary**
> rustling: *dry sound of cloth, paper or leaves*
> drifts: *moves aimlessly*
> foot-fall: *footsteps*
> scurry: *run*
> rejoicer: *one who makes glad*
> clings: *holds tightly, sticks*

a) Of the five senses (touch, taste, smell, hearing, sight), which are used in this poem?
b) What exactly is meant by 'she . . . is beneath them'?
   – she's lying on the ground, covered in leaves
   – she's fallen asleep in the garden
   – she's in the cellar

– she's dead
– she's sweeping the leaves in the courtyard.
c) What is the connection between 'she' and 'a wet leaf'? How are they similar?
d) What feelings does this poem communicate to you? Are they named in the poem?

11 'Liu Ch'e' is an adaptation of a much older Chinese poem. Here is another of Pound's Chinese adaptations, followed by a note supplied by the poet. Read the poem and note carefully, comparing the two.

The Jewel Stairs' Grievance

The jewelled steps are already quite white with dew,
It is so late that the dew soaks my gauze stockings,
And I let down the crystal curtain
And watch the moon through the clear autumn.

Note – Jewel stairs, therefore a palace. Grievance, therefore there is something to complain of. Gauze stockings, therefore a court lady, not a servant who complains. Clear autumn, therefore he has no excuse on account of the weather. Also she has come early, for the dew has not merely whitened the stairs, but has soaked her stockings. The poem is especially prized because she utters no direct reproach.

Ezra Pound

The art of such poems is to express emotion indirectly – without naming it. A scene is described in almost entirely physical terms (one could easily imagine it as a film-sequence), yet an emotional dimension is created when the poem is sensitively read. This is because the physical details are carefully selected to suggest precise secondary meanings.

12 Try to write a note, similar to Pound's, for the poem 'Liu Ch'e'.

13 Read this poem by John Masefield. As you read, try to guess the meaning of the title: who or what is C.L.M.? And how old is the man who is speaking?

C.L.M.

In the dark womb where I began
My mother's life made me a man.
Through all the months of human birth
Her beauty fed my common earth.
5 I cannot see, nor breathe, nor stir,
But through the death of some of her.

> **Vocabulary**
> womb: *part of the woman's body where a foetus grows*
> common: *ordinary*
> stir: *move*

Down in the darkness of the grave
She cannot see the life she gave.
For all her love, she cannot tell
10 Whether I use it ill or well,
Nor knock at dusty doors to find
Her beauty dusty in the mind.

If the grave's gates could be undone,
She would not know her little son,
15 I am so grown. If we should meet
She would pass by me in the street,
Unless my soul's face let her see
My sense of what she did for me.

What have I done to keep in mind
20 My debt to her and womankind?
What woman's happier life repays
Her for those months of wretched days?
For all my mouthless body leeched
Ere Birth's releasing hell was reached?

25 What have I done, or tried, or said
In thanks to that dear woman dead?
Men triumph over woman still,
Men trample women's rights at will,
And man's lust roves the world untamed.

30 O grave, keep shut lest I be shamed.

John Masefield

> ill: *badly*
> keep in mind: *remember*
> wretched: *miserable*
> leeched: *sucked*
> ere: *(archaic) before*
> trample: *walk on; disregard*
> lust: *powerful sexual desire
> (traditionally, one of the 'seven
> deadly sins')*
> roves: *moves freely around*
> untamed: *uncontrolled; wild*

Close reading

14 Match the following summaries with the stanzas of the poem:

Stanza No.

I've done nothing to help women   _____
My mother wouldn't recognize me now   _____
The price of my life was hers   _____
Have I repaid her for what she gave?   _____
She's gone for ever   _____

15 Find the phrases or sentences in the poem that correspond to the
following:
  a) man's entry into the world is a moment of torment
  b) women are treated as instruments for the relief of sexual
  drives

c) it may be that one's thoughts and feelings are somehow visible to others
d) the political status of women is unequal
e) the basic physical constituents of a human being were made into something beautiful by her
f) women suffer humiliation by men
g) she cannot even speak to people who remember her as she was in her finest years
h) have I paid back my debt by making another woman happy?
i) if it were possible for the dead to return to life

16 Compare this poem to 'Sindhi Woman' and 'Liu Ch'e' in the following terms:
a) the description of each woman
b) the poet's presentation of himself
c) the poem's moral (if it has one)
d) the image of woman that results.

Language practice – structures

Purpose clauses

a) What have I done *to keep in mind*
   My debt to her and womankind?
b) O grave, keep shut *lest I be shamed*.

The phrases in italics both express a purpose, but in b) the purpose is negative. Note: *lest* is not much used in modern spoken English, although it can still be found in writing. Instead of *lest*, we generally use one of the following structures:

1) *so as not to* . . . + infinitive
2) *so that* . . . *not* . . . + present, future, or conditional

Examples
1) She came in quietly *so as not to* wake the children.
2) He closed the curtains *so that* the neighbours would*n't* see him.

17 Complete the following sentences using purpose clauses:
a) The Sindhi woman walks smoothly / jar / not fall from her head.
b) Pound used symbols / not / express emotion directly.
c) In 'The Jewel Stairs' Grievance' the woman goes out / look for her lover.
d) Masefield probably wrote 'C.L.M.' / expiate feelings of guilt towards his mother.

   e) He wants his mother to remain in her grave / she / not see
        how little he has done to thank her.

18 Now re-write sentences a), b), e), in question 17 using *avoid* or
     prevent.

Examples
   1) She came in quietly to *avoid* waking the children.
   2) He closed the curtains to *prevent* the neighbours seeing him.

19 Here is a list of practical measures taken by women in the last
     twenty years to put an end to their dominance by men.
   a) They call themselves 'Ms' instead of 'Mrs' or 'Miss'.
   b) They organize crèches [nurseries for young children] at their
        places of work.
   c) They go to self-defence classes.
   d) They set up 'Well Women Clinics' staffed by women doctors.
   e) They don't wear make-up.
   f) They ask their partners to help with housework.
   g) They don't get married.
   h) They keep separate bank accounts from their partners.
   Say what the purpose of each of these measures is, using the
   structures practised in this section.

20 Can you think of any more things women have done to help
     themselves? Do you have any ideas for what else they could do?
     In each case, write down the purpose of each action.

Vocabulary

21 Which of the following words are most appropriate to describe
     the poet's feelings towards the women in each of the poems?
     (Look up any words you don't know, and note that more than one
     word may be suitable for each poem.)

love	*arrogance*	*regret*
sexual attraction	*pity*	*embarrassment*
admiration	*guilt*	*joy*
humility	*sorrow*	
contempt	*amazement*	
envy	*compassion*	
shame	*excitement*	
surprise	*reverence*	
affection	*fear*	
nostalgia	*anger*	
awe	*condescension*	

The fathers with broad belts under their suits
And seamy foreheads; mothers loud and fat;
An uncle shouting smut; and then the perms,
The nylon gloves and jewellery-substitutes,
40 The lemons, mauves, and olive-ochres that

Marked off the girls unreally from the rest.
   Yes, from cafés
And banquet-halls up yards, and bunting-dressed
Coach-party annexes, the wedding-days
45 Were coming to an end. All down the line
Fresh couples climbed aboard: the rest stood round;
The last confetti and advice were thrown,
And, as we moved, each face seemed to define
Just what it saw departing: children frowned
50 At something dull; fathers had never known

Success so huge and wholly farcical;
   The women shared
The secret like a happy funeral;
While girls, gripping their handbags tighter, stared
55 At a religious wounding. Free at last,
And loaded with the sum of all they saw,
We hurried towards London, shuffling gouts of steam.
Now fields were building-plots, and poplars cast
Long shadows over major roads, and for
60 Some fifty minutes, that in time would seem

Just long enough to settle hats and say
   I nearly died,
A dozen marriages got under way.
They watched the landscape, sitting side by side
65 —An Odeon went past, a cooling tower,
And someone running up to bowl – and none
Thought of the others they would never meet
Or how their lives would all contain this hour.
I thought of London spread out in the sun,
70 Its postal districts packed like squares of wheat:

There we were aimed. And as we raced across
   Bright knots of rail
Past standing Pullmans, walls of blackened moss
Came close, and it was nearly done, this frail
75 Travelling coincidence; and what it held
Stood ready to be loosed with all the power
That being changed can give. We slowed again,
And as the tightened brakes took hold, there swelled
A sense of falling, like an arrow-shower
80 Sent out of sight, somewhere becoming rain.

Philip Larkin

seamy: *literally, with the seams (stitching) visible; therefore, deeply lined and/or rather ugly*
smut: *sexual jokes (literally: dirt)*
perm: *'permanent wave' hairstyle*
lemons, mauves, olive-ochres: *typical restrained colours of English clothes*

bunting: *flags of celebration*
coach-party annexes: *extra rooms in pubs for groups travelling in coaches*
confetti: *little pieces of coloured paper thrown over bride and groom at weddings*

farcical: *like a farce (exaggerated theatrical comedy)*
gripping: *holding tightly*
shuffling: *mixing or pushing*
gouts: *large sudden splashes*
poplars: *trees of the genus Populus*
major roads: *main roads*
wounding (wu:nding): *injury in which the skin is cut or penetrated*

got under way: *began their journey*
Odeon: *cinema*
cooling tower: *large concrete tower for cooling water at power-stations*
running up to bowl: *part of the game of cricket*

Pullmans: *restaurant or sleeping carriages*
done: *finished*
frail: *delicate, easily broken*
loosed: *released*
swelled: *grew*
arrow-shower: *many arrows shot simultaneously, with an effect like a shower.*

'Sindhi Woman'
'Liu Ch'e'
'C.L.M.'

22 Write some sentences comparing the feelings expressed in the three poems.

Extension

23 Do you think the following is still true?

Men triumph over women still,
Men trample women's rights at will,
And man's lust roves the world untamed.

Write a short essay in response.

Beyond the text

24 Read these two poems and say whether you think each was written by a man or a woman. Give reasons for your opinion.

The Mutes

Those groans men use
passing a woman on the street
or on the steps of the subway

to tell her she is a female
5 and their flesh knows it,

are they a sort of tune,
an ugly enough song, sung
by a bird with a slit tongue

but meant for music?

10 Or are they the muffled roaring
of deaf mutes trapped in a building that is
slowly filling with smoke?

Perhaps both.

Such men most often
15 look as if groan were all they could do,
yet a woman, in spite of herself,

Vocabulary
mute: *person who cannot speak*
slit: *cut*
muffled: *suppressed*
deaf mute: *person who cannot
hear or speak*

knows it's a tribute:
if she were lacking all grace
they'd pass her in silence:

20 so it's not only to say she's
a warm hole. It's a word

in grief-language, nothing to do with
primitive, not an ur-language;
language stricken, sickened, cast down

25 in decrepitude. She wants to
throw the tribute away, dis-
gusted, and can't,

it goes on buzzing in her ear,
it changes the pace of her walk,
30 the torn posters in echoing corridors

spell it out, it
quakes and gnashes as the train comes in.
Her pulse sullenly

had picked up speed,
35 but the cars slow down and
jar to a stop while her understanding

keeps on translating:
'Life after life after life goes by

without poetry,
40 without seemliness,
without love.'

> ur-language: *'ur-' is a German*
> *prefix meaning 'original' or*
> *'primitive'*
> stricken: *wounded (physically or*
> *emotionally)*
> decrepitude: *extreme weakness*
> *of old age*
> quake: *shake violently*
> gnash: *grind the teeth (usually*
> *in anger or pain)*
> jar: *bang*
> seemliness: *beauty; respectful*
> *behaviour*

Daphne Morse

I'd not thought of her for twenty years
except from time to time, coming across
the old snap of us at Scarborough,
its yellowed monochrome
5 showing us both laughing on the beach,
my springing red hair printed as dark
as her lustrous black.

Daphne Morse. We were always laughing together,
seeing façades as faces, windows as eyes,
10 sharing jokes and confidences.
And how we admired each other! And sought
adventure, making aimless journeys,
lodging in attics and cottages, discovering
high moors in the short summer.

> **Vocabulary**
> snap: *photograph*
> Scarborough: *a seaside resort in*
> *Yorkshire, N. England*
> printed: *in the photograph*
> lustrous: *full of lustre, shiny*
> façade: *the front of a building*

15 It was so long ago, her death,
the scar of it healed, faded;
and yet today unreasonably, unprompted,
I ve grieved with a clear bitterness
for her, shortlived
20 and lovely Daphne Morse.
Thought how her cheeks bloomed
and her throat was smooth
and so were mine, bloomy, smooth.

The looking-glass
25 is half my present grief.

> bloomy: *full of bloom (healthy red colour; also perfection, delicate beauty)*
> looking-glass: *mirror*

Authors

Jon Stallworthy was born in London in 1935 and studied at Oxford. He served in the Army from 1953 to 1955, and worked in publishing from 1959 to 1977. He worked for some time as a representative of Oxford University Press in Pakistan. Since 1977 he has taught English at Oxford and Cornell Universities. He has published several volumes of verse, studies of Yeats and Wilfred Owen, and edited *The Penguin Book of Love Poetry* and *The Oxford Book of War Poetry*.

Ezra Pound (1885-1972) was born in Idaho, and studied at Hamilton College, Pennsylvania. After a short unhappy spell of teaching in Indiana he left the USA in 1908 and moved to Europe. Pound quickly became one of the most influential and dynamic figures in literary London. He was a key figure in the Modernist movement, and, as T S Eliot said, 'more responsible for the 20th Century revolution in poetry than any other individual'. In 1920 he moved to Paris, and in 1925 to Rapallo, in Italy. Here he became increasingly involved in bizarre economic theories, leading him to adopt anti-semitic, pro-fascist views. During the war he produced radio propaganda for Mussolini, and in 1945 was arrested and tried for treason. His life was saved by a successful plea of insanity, but he was forced to spend the next 13 years in a mental hospital. In 1958 he was released, and moved back to Italy. He is buried in Venice.

Pound was a keen translator of Greek, Anglo-Saxon, Italian, Chinese and Provençal poetry, believing that the greatest examples of these literatures were neglected in England and America in the early years of this century, and that poetry in English could be given new vigour through the study of their poetic techniques. Interestingly, in 'Liu Ch'e', and a later collection called *Cathay*, Pound did not work from Chinese originals (he did not understand Chinese), but from literal translations made by others. Often his adaptations are very free, and their inaccuracies have aroused the criticism of scholars. This does not, of course, prevent a number of them being very fine English poems in their own right.

John Masefield (1878-1967) was born in Herefordshire. After his mother's death in 1884 he was brought up by relatives. After school, he became a sailor, but after four years left the sea and wandered around the USA, taking odd jobs and writing poetry. He returned to England and published his first book of poems, *Salt-Water Ballads*, in 1902. Over the next 65 years he published another 50 volumes of poetry, 20 novels and 8 plays. He became Poet Laureate in 1930, and is best remembered now for his children's stories and a number of jaunty sea-poems such as 'Cargoes'. He also wrote two autobiographical works: *So Long to Learn*, and *Grace before Ploughing*.

5 Love

Au Clair de la Lune
by Ethel Gabain
(Victorian and Albert Museum)

Before you read

1   The word 'love' is one of the most difficult words to define, even though it is one of the commonest human feelings. Here are some possible uses of the word, and some definitions.

Uses

1   Love your neighbour as you love yourself

2   William and Anne are in love

3   A mother's love for her child

Definitions

A   An intense enjoyment

B   A mixture of obligation, affection and respect

C   A passionate attachment, usually accompanied by sexual desire

Uses

4 A child's love for its mother

5 Harry loves chocolate cake

6 They loved each other like brothers

7 He loves his country more than his own life

8 A man's love for his parents

9 The love of two people married for 20 years

Definition

D A feeling of comfort and security

E Deep satisfaction in the happiness of another

F Dedication to something greater than oneself

G An intense form of friendship

H Affection based on long acquaintance

I A powerful protective feeling

a) Match each use with an appropriate definition.
   1 ___ 2 ___ 3 ___ 4 ___ 5 ___ 6 ___ 7 ___ 8 ___ 9 ___
b) Can any of these definitions fit more than one use?
c) Can you think of any other possible uses of the word 'love'?
d) Divide the uses of 'love' listed above into *selfish* and *unselfish* feelings. Are any of the feelings difficult to place in one category or the other?

2 Read 'The Voice' by Rupert Brooke and complete the sentences:
a) The three things loved by the poet are

_____

_____

_____

b) 'The voice' of the title belongs to

_____

The Voice

Safe in the magic of my woods
   I lay, and watched the dying light.
Faint in the pale high solitudes,
   And washed with rain and veiled by night,

5 Silver and blue and green were showing.
   And the dark woods grew darker still;
And birds were hushed; and peace was growing;
   And quietness crept up the hill;

And no wind was blowing . . .

10 And I knew
That this was the hour of knowing,
And the night and the woods and you

> **Vocabulary**
> veiled: *lightly covered*
> hushed: *silent*
> crept: *moved quietly*

Were one together, and I should find
Soon in the silence the hidden key
15 Of all that had hurt and puzzled me –
Why you were you, and the night was kind,
And the woods were part of the heart of me.

And there I waited breathlessly,
Alone; and slowly the holy three,
20 The three that I loved, together grew
One, in the hour of knowing,
Night, and the woods, and you –

And suddenly
There was an uproar in my woods,
25 The noise of a fool in mock distress,
Crashing and laughing and blindly going,
Of ignorant feet and a swishing dress,
And a Voice profaning the solitudes.

The spell was broken, the key denied me,
30 And at length your flat clear voice beside me
Mouthed cheerful clear flat platitudes.

You came and quacked beside me in the wood.
You said, 'The view from here is very good!'
You said, 'It's nice to be alone a bit!'
35 And, 'How the days are drawing out!' you said.
You said, 'The sunset's pretty, isn't it?'

By God! I wish – I wish that you were dead!

Rupert Brooke

breathlessly: *as if without breathing*
uproar: *loud noise*
mock: *false, joking*
crashing: *making loud noises*
swish: *noise of cloth, grass, etc moving*
profane: *do something vulgar or offensive in a holy place*
spell: *magic*
platitudes: *commonplace remarks*
quack: *the noise of a duck*
draw out: *grow longer*

First reaction

3   Why do you think the poet says 'I wish that you were dead'?

Close reading

4   Which of the definitions of love given above in **1** would you
apply to the poet's feeling towards
a) night?
b) the woods?
c) you?

5   Here is a brief summary of the poem. Fill in the line numbers corresponding to the five sections:

Description of the scene   Line _____ to line _____

The poet's state of mind   Line _____ to line _____

An interruption   Line _____ to line _____

A trite conversation   Line _____ to line _____

Final reaction   Line _____ to line _____

6   Comprehension questions:
   a)   Why is there 'magic' in the woods (line 1)?
   b)   'the hour of knowing' (line 11) – knowing what?
   c)   'all that had hurt and puzzled me' (line 15) – what do you think the poet is referring to?
   d)   'the night was kind' (line 16) – in what sense can a night be 'kind'?
   e)   'I waited breathlessly' (line 18) – what does this mean?
   f)   'the holy three . . . together grew one' (lines 19-21) – Can you explain this phrase?
   g)   'ignorant feet' (line 27) – what does this mean?
   h)   'The spell was broken' (line 29) – What 'spell' is this?
   i)   'quacked' (line 32) – What does this suggest about the lover?
   j)   'I wish that you were dead!' (line 37) – Is this literally true, do you think? If not, what is the meaning?

7 **a)**   The phrase 'my woods' is used twice in the poem (lines 1 and 24). Write down any other words that are repeated (there are at least 12).
   b)   Is the poem
      i)   metrical with a regular rhyme-scheme?
      ii)   metrical but unrhymed?
      iii)   neither metrical nor rhymed (free verse)?
      iv)   partly metrical, with an irregular rhyme-scheme?
   c)   What is the effect of the two short lines in the poem (lines 10 and 23)?
   d)   Can you think of any ways in which the form of the poem reflects its content?

8   From the list, choose two adjectives to describe the poet's relationship with each of the following:

a)   nature _____

b)   the lover _____

c)   himself _____

Adjectives	
reverent	dismissive
analytical	confused
turbulent	calm
violent	tender
aggressive	benign
condescending	tolerant
appreciative	irritable

9   In your own words, give a short summary (maximum 35 words) of what happens in the poem.

Read the following poem.

When You Died

1

When you died
I went through the rain
Carrying my nightmare
To register the death.

5 A well-groomed healthy gentleman
Safe within his office
Said – Are you the widow?

Couldn't he have said
Were you his wife?

2

10 After the first shock
I found I was
Solidly set in my flesh.
I was an upright central pillar,
The soft flesh melted round me.
15 My eyes melted
Spilling the inexhaustible essence of sorrow.
The soft flesh of the body
Melted onto chairs and into beds
Dragging its emptiness and pain.

20 I lodged inside holding myself upright,
Warding off the dreadful deliquescence.

3

November.
Stooping under muslins
Of grey rain I fingered
25 Through ribbons of wet grass,
Traced stiff stems down to the wormy earth
And one by one snapped off
The pale surviving flowers; they would ride
With him, lie on the polished plank
30 Above his breast.

People said – Why do you not
Follow the coffin?
Why do you not

Vocabulary
register: *inform the municipal authorities*
well-groomed: *with a very neat hairstyle*

lodged: *stayed*
warding off: *keeping away*
deliquescence: *process of becoming liquid*

muslins: *thin cotton cloths*
wormy: *full of worms*
snapped: *broke*
plank: *flat piece of wood (part of the coffin)*

Have any funeral words spoken?
35 Why not
Send flowers from a shop?

4

When you died
They burnt you.
They brought home to me
40 A vase of thin metal;
Inside, a plasty bag
Crammed, full of gritty pieces.
Ground bones, not silky ash.

Where shall I put this substance?
45 Shall I scatter it
With customary thoughts
Of nature's mystical balance
Among the roses?

Shall I disperse it into the winds
50 That blow across Cambeake Cliff
Or drop it on to places where you
Lived, worked, were happy?

Finally shall I perhaps keep it
Which after all was you
55 Quietly on a shelf
And when I follow
My old grit can lie
No matter where with yours
Slowly sinking into the earth together.

plasty: *plastic*
crammed: *pushed in*
gritty: *like grit (very small
stones)*
ground: *past participle of* grind
Cambeake Cliff: *a headland
near Boscastle, Cornwall,
England*

5

60 When you died
I did not for the moment
Think about myself;
I grieved deeply and purely for your loss,
That you had lost your life.
65 I grieved bitterly for your mind destroyed,
Your courage thrown away,
Your senses aborted under the amazing skin
No one would ever touch again.

I grieve still
70 That we'd have grown
Even more deeply close and old together
And now shall not.

grieved: *felt intense sorrow*
aborted: *prematurely killed*

Pamela Gillilan

First reaction

10 What do you think might be the answer to the three questions asked in lines 31-36?

Close reading

11 Read lines 5-9 again. What is the difference between the two questions 'Were you his wife?' and 'Are you the widow?'? Why does she prefer one to the other?

12 In section 2 there are many references to 'melting' and similar sensations. The most obvious interpretation is that the woman cried a lot (lines 15-16); but what about line 14 and lines 17-21? What is she describing here?

13 In section 3, the poet describes picking wild flowers to put on her lover's coffin instead of sending flowers from a shop. Can you suggest an explanation for this?

14 'Where shall I put this substance?' (line 44). Which of the four actions that follow do you think she is *least* likely to take? Why? Which do you think she is *most* likely to take?

15 'When You Died' contains several details which add to the poem's meaning by suggestion. An example is the 'gentleman' in line 5 whose health and care for his hair contrast poignantly with the dead lover who has neither health nor hair any longer. Can you explain the suggestions contained in the following details – 'rain' (lines 2, 24) 'wormy earth' (26) 'surviving' (28) 'thin metal' (40) 'ground bones, not silky ash' (43) 'amazing skin' (67)?

16 Look back to question 7(b). Which of the four categories listed there fit this poem? In what way is this form suitable for this poem?

17 Which of the definitions of 'love' in the first section of this chapter best describes the feelings expressed by the poet towards her husband?

18 What other feelings do you find in this poem?

Language practice – structures

19 Put the following into reported speech:
  a) A gentleman said – Are you the widow?
  b) People said – Why do you not follow the coffin?
  c) People said – Why do you not have any funeral words spoken?
  d) People said – Why not send flowers from a shop?
  e) She asked herself 'Where shall I put this substance?'
  f) She asked herself 'Shall I scatter it among the roses?'
  g) She asked herself 'Shall I disperse it into the winds?'
  h) She reflected, 'We'd have grown old together if he'd lived, but now we shan't.'

20 Use the reporting verbs given in brackets to put the following into reported speech.
  a) You said, 'The view from here is very good!' (drew his attention)
  b) You said, 'It's nice to be alone a bit!' (remarked)
  c) 'How the days are drawing out!' you said. (observed)
  d) You said, 'The sunset's pretty, isn't it?'(pointed out)

21 Complete these sentences about 'The Voice':
  a) Brooke / seem / believe / magic / woods
  b) Brooke / sensitive / colours / effects / evening light
  c) Brooke / expect / find / key / pain / silence
  d) Brooke / describe / three loves/ one
  e) Brooke / see / lover's platitudes / act of profanation.

22 Complete these sentences about 'When You Died':
  a) Gillilan / not / seem / believe / religion / help her.
  b) Gillilan / sensitive / textures / physical world
  c) Gillilan / not / expect / find / consolation / anything
  d) Gillilan / describe / detail / experience / grief
  e) Gillilan / see / death / husband / waste / something beautiful

23 Write a short comparison of the attitudes expressed in the two poems towards annoying voices. Use these notes to help you:
  Brooke: lover's voice a profanation – destroys magic. Wants solitude, silence. Lover speaks platitudes.
  Gillilan: voices of others a disturbance – questions about flowers, funeral speeches.
  Both: silence best at times of intense emotion.

Vocabulary

24 a) Pick out all the words that refer to noise (or absence of noise) in 'The Voice'.

b) List them in order of loudness:

silent		
1	7	
2	8	
3	9	
4	10	
5	11	
6	loud	

c) List in order of loudness the following words describing the intensity of sound
deafening / distant / barely audible / ear-splitting / faint / clear / loud / soft

silent		
1	5	
2	6	
3	7	
4	8	
	loud	

25 Choose the noise to go with the definition:

Definitions   Noises
The sound of . . .

		Noises
a) a glass breaking	_____	crunch
b) someone walking on gravel	_____	smash
c) someone turning the pages of a newspaper	_____	splash
d) someone jumping into a swimming pool	_____	screech
e) a strong wind	_____	lapping
f) a bird singing	_____	drumming
g) a low-flying jet aircraft	_____	clatter
h) a car taking a corner too fast	_____	twitter
i) rain on a metal roof	_____	howl
j) waves breaking gently on a shore	_____	roar
k) a bee flying	_____	rustle
l) a door shutting violently	_____	rumble
m) a hinge that needs oiling	_____	bang
n) someone typing quickly	_____	buzz
o) thunder	_____	creak

26 **a)** Some of the sounds listed above are traditionally thought of as *soothing*, others as more *disturbing*. Which would you put in each category?

   b) Now put them in the categories *romantic / banal*.

   c) Have you put the same words in the categories *soothing* and *romantic*? If not, can you explain why?

27 Translate the 'noise' words above into your own language.
In English, most 'noise' words are *onomatopoeic* (ie their sound imitates their meaning). They can also be used either as nouns or as verbs. Is this true of your language too?

28 Which of the 'noise' words in 'The Voice' are onomatopoeic?

29 Write down any more 'noise' words you can think of in your own language, and find the English equivalents in a dictionary.

Extension

30 Is there a poem about love in your language that you particularly like? What kinds of love does it describe? Does it have any similarities with either of the poems in this chapter?

Beyond the text

Here is a poem by Thomas Hardy: 'At Castle Boterel'. It describes a visit that Hardy made as an old man (aged 73) to Boscastle in Cornwall. Here, 43 years previously, he had walked with the girl who was to become his wife. Now, in 1913, his wife is dead; yet he seems to see her (and himself) as they were in their youth, climbing the same hill out of the town. 'Was there ever,' he asks, 'A time of such quality, since or before, / In that hill's story?'; and replies 'To one mind never'. He claims also that the rocks by the roadside 'record' the passing of the two lovers.

   When you have read the poem, answer the following questions:

31 What do you think of these claims? How would you describe the philosophy of love that Hardy is expressing here?

At Castle Boterel

As I drive to the junction of lane and highway,
    And the drizzle bedrenches the waggonette,
I look behind at the fading byway,
    And see on its slope, now glistening wet,
5   Distinctly yet

Myself and a girlish form benighted
    In dry March weather. We climb the road
Beside a chaise. We had just alighted
    To ease the sturdy pony's load
10   When he sighed and slowed.

What we did as we climbed, and what we talked of
    Matters not much, nor to what it led, –
Something that life will not be balked of
    Without rude reason till hope is dead,
15   And feeling fled.

It filled but a minute. But was there ever
    A time of such quality, since or before,
In that hill's story? To one mind never,
    Though it has been climbed, foot-swift, foot-sore,
20   By thousands more.

Primaeval rocks form the road's steep border,
    And much have they faced there, first and last,
Of the transitory in Earth's long order;
    But what they record in colour and cast
25   Is – that we two passed.

And to me, though Time's unflinching rigour,
    In mindless rote, has ruled from sight
The substance now, one phantom figure
    Remains on the slope, as when that night
30   Saw us alight.

I look and see it there, shrinking, shrinking,
    I look back at it amid the rain
For the very last time; for my sand is sinking,
    And I shall traverse old love's domain
35   Never again.

Thomas Hardy

Vocabulary
drizzle: *light, steady rain*
bedrenches: *wets*
waggonette: *a four-wheeled carriage pulled by horses*
byway: *a small road (lane)*
slope: *hill*
glistening: *softly and wetly shining*
benighted: *overtaken by darkness*
chaise: *a light horse-drawn carriage*
sturdy: *strongly-built*
balked of: *denied, prevented from having*
rude: *rough, violent*
fled: *gone*
something . . . feeling fled: *the general meaning is 'something that life must have, as long as people continue to hope and feel'*
foot-swift: *walking quickly*
foot-sore: *walking painfully*
transitory: *not enduring, short-lived*
order: *sequence of events (ie history)*
cast: *form*
unflinching: *to flinch is to turn away with pain or pity; unflinching is the opposite (pitiless)*
rigour: *strictness in applying a law, severity*
rote: *routine action*
ruled from sight: *cancelled, removed*
substance: *the physical person*
alight: *step off a vehicle*
my sand is sinking: *my time is running out*
traverse: *cross.*

Authors

Rupert Brooke (1887-1915) was born and educated in Rugby, then at Cambridge, where he was the leading poet of his time. He became a celebrated literary figure in the years before World War I, and a popular symbol of patriotism through his war poems of 1914. On his way to fight in the Dardanelles he died of septicaemia on the Greek island of Skyros in 1915.

Pamela Gillilan was born in London and, after marrying, moved to Cornwall. She began to write poetry (after a 25-year silence) when her husband died. She has published two books of poems, *That Winter* (1986) (nominated for the Commonwealth Poetry Prize) and *The Turnspit Dog* (1991).

Thomas Hardy (1840-1928) was born and educated in Dorset. He trained and worked as an architect, first in London, then in Dorchester. While restoring the church of St. Juliot, near Boscastle in Cornwall, he fell in love with the vicar's sister-in-law, and later married her (1874). In the same year, with the success of his novel, *Far from the Madding Crowd*, he took up writing full-time. Although his marriage was not happy, the death of his wife in 1912 triggered an extraordinary series of love-poems, among them 'At Castle Boterel'. Hardy is unique in being one of the greatest of England's novelists and short-story writers as well as one of her finest poets.

6 Trains

Before you read

1 Look carefully at the photograph on the next page and say
   a) what you see in it.
   b) what you imagine the photographer wants you to feel as you look at the picture
   c) how closely this image of rail travel corresponds to your experiences of trains.

2 Read this poem, and say which of the senses (hearing, sight, smell etc) the poem uses most effectively to convey the experience described.

Adlestrop

Yes. I remember Adlestrop –
The name, because one afternoon
Of heat the express-train drew up there
Unwontedly. It was late June.

5 The steam hissed. Someone cleared his throat.
No one left and no one came
On the bare platform. What I saw
Was Adlestrop – only the name

And willows, willow-herb, and grass,
10 And meadowsweet, and haycocks dry,
No whit less still and lonely fair
Than the high cloudlets in the sky.

And for that minute a blackbird sang
Close by, and round him, mistier,
15 Farther and farther, all the birds
Of Oxfordshire and Gloucestershire.

Edward Thomas

> **Vocabulary**
> Adlestrop: *a small (now disused) station in Gloucestershire, on the line from Oxford to Worcester*
> unwontedly: *unusually*
> cleared his throat: *gave a small cough*
> willows: *trees of the genus Salix which grow near rivers*
> willow-herb: *a tall, pink-petalled wild flower (Epilobium)*
> meadowsweet: *a wild flower with creamy yellow petals, (Filipendula)*
> haycocks: *conical stacks of cut grass*
> no whit less . . . than: *just as . . . as*
> fair: *beautiful*
> cloudlets: *small clouds*
> blackbird: *a black species of thrush (Merula turdus), very common in England, celebrated for its song*
> mistier: *comparative of* misty *(indistinct, as when there is mist in the air).*

Ribblehead Viaduct by Denis Thorpe 1986 (The Guardian)

First reaction

3 How important is the train in this poem? Would anything be lost if the poet described himself arriving by bicycle? Or in a car?

4 Read this poem. (Don't be put off by the length, or by phrases that seem difficult to understand. This is one of the great poems of the last 50 years – take it slowly, and enjoy it!)

The Whitsun Weddings

That Whitsun, I was late getting away:
   Not till about
One-twenty on the sunlit Saturday
Did my three-quarters-empty train pull out,
5 All windows down, all cushions hot, all sense
Of being in a hurry gone. We ran
Behind the backs of houses, crossed a street
Of blinding windscreens, smelt the fish-dock; thence
The river's level drifting breadth began,
10 Where sky and Lincolnshire and water meet.

All afternoon, through the tall heat that slept
   For miles inland,
A slow and stopping curve southwards we kept.
Wide farms went by, short-shadowed cattle, and
15 Canals with floatings of industrial froth;
A hothouse flashed uniquely: hedges dipped
And rose: and now and then a smell of grass
Displaced the reek of buttoned carriage-cloth
Until the next town, new and nondescript,
20 Approached with acres of dismantled cars.

At first, I didn't notice what a noise
   The weddings made
Each station that we stopped at: sun destroys
The interest of what's happening in the shade,
25 And down the long cool platforms whoops and skirls
I took for porters larking with the mails,
And went on reading. Once we started, though,
We passed them, grinning and pomaded, girls
In parodies of fashion, heels and veils,
30 All posed irresolutely, watching us go,

As if out on the end of an event
   Waving goodbye
To something that survived it. Struck, I leant
More promptly out next time, more curiously,
35 And saw it all again in different terms:

Vocabulary
Whitsun: *short for Whit Sunday or Whitsuntide, the religious feast of Pentecost, on the 7th Sunday after Easter.*
pull out: *leave the station*
fish-dock: *Larkin worked in Hull, a fishing-port in Yorkshire*
river: *the river Humber*
Lincolnshire: *the next county south from Hull*

floatings: *pieces of floating matter*
froth: *mass of bubbles*
hothouse: *glass structure for growing tropical plants or early vegetables*
uniquely: *in a unique way; or once*
dipped: *went down*
reek: *strong, bitter smell*
carriage-cloth: *the cloth of the seats in the railway carriage*
nondescript: *with nothing special about it; dull*
acres: *large areas of land (1 acre = 4,046.9 square metres)*
dismantled: *broken down into pieces*

whoops: *[onomatopoeia] shouts of excitement*
skirls: *shrill cries*
took for: *interpreted as*
larking: *playing like children*
mails: *post-bags*
grinning: *with big smiles*
pomaded: *perfumed*
heels: *shoes with high heels*
veils: *fine cloth or net hiding the face (part of a bride's costume)*
posed: *standing for photographs*
irresolute: *with no intention in mind*

struck: *curiosity aroused*
promptly: *quickly*

First reaction

5   'Post-war provincial England in all its dreariness'

(A. Alvarez)

'a concluding stanza ... delicately poised between hope and failure'

(Michael Kirkham)

'I remember Larkin writing to tell me, when I was about to produce the first broadcast reading ... of 'The Whitsun Weddings', that what I should aim to get from the actor was a level, even plodding, descriptive note, until the mysterious last lines, when the poem should suddenly 'lift off the ground.'

(Anthony Thwaite)

What do you sense at the end of this poem – Hope? Mystery? Failure? Or a delicate balance between them?

Close reading

6   **a)**   What is the chronological structure of this poem? Write down the numbers of the lines that describe the following stages of the journey:

  1 Departure from Hull   Lines _____

  2 The first part of the journey   Lines _____

  3 The central part of the journey   Lines _____

  4 The final part of the journey   Lines _____

  5 Arrival in London   Lines _____

  b)   Where do the stages of the journey correspond to the division of the poem into stanzas?

  c)   Why do you think the poet made more than half the poem 'overflow' the stanza divisions?

   i)   Because he couldn't make it fit.

   ii)   Because poetic thought always overflows metrical forms.

   iii) Because the start and end of any journey are 'tidy' times; the middle is usually formless.

   iv)   Because the poet's thoughts about the weddings 'overflow' the occasion.

7   **a)**   Who do the following refer to?

   'them' (line 28) 'their' (line 68) 'it' (line 33) 'we' (line 71) 'it' (line 35) 'it' (line 75) 'they' (line 64)

     b) Whose 'faces' are described in line 48 – the passengers on the train, or the people on the station platform?

     c) Who is 'loaded' and who are 'they' in line 56?

8 Find the metaphors and similes in the poem (see Chapter 3 *Images* if you are uncertain about these terms) in which the following associations are made:

     a) the weather – a living creature

     b) a city – fields of grain

     c) railway lines – ropes or cables

     d) marriage – death

9   The women shared
       The secret like a happy funeral (lines 52-53)

     a) What is 'the secret'?

     b) Why do you think the poet uses the word 'funeral'? Who (or what) has died?

     c) Why is the funeral 'happy'?

10 What do you understand by the words 'a religious wounding' in line 55?

11   there swelled
       A sense of falling, like an arrow-shower
       Sent out of sight, somewhere becoming rain. (78-80)

     a) What associations or connotations do the words 'swelled', 'falling', 'arrow', 'shower' and 'rain' have for you? Write down as many of these associations as you can think of below:

swelled	falling	arrow	shower	rain

(Note: for another use of the word 'shower' see Edward Thomas's poem 'Tall Nettles', page 38. For 'rain' see also Pamela Gillilan, 'When You Died', pages 59-60.)

     b) What similarities can you find between the connotations of these words?

     c) What clashes or oppositions can you find between the connotations of these words?

     d) What complex of ideas is produced by the image 'arrow-shower'?

     e) What sort of 'rain' would an 'arrow-shower' become? Is there any hope in this image or is it simply full of death?

12 Read the poem again, and pick out all the images that seem to you to imply (a) hope, (b) failure or despair, (c) an ambiguous position between the two.

Which category is most numerous – a, b or c? Which seems to you most important in the poem?

13 Do you think that hope and failure are the two most important feelings in this poem, or should we look for other things?

14 If you read the account of Pentecost in the Bible (Acts of the Apostles, 1-2), you find that Jesus makes the following promise to his disciples before going up into the sky: 'You shall receive power, after the Holy Spirit has come upon you.' A few days later, this 'power' is given to them in a dramatic scene in which the Holy Spirit appears with a sound of rushing wind, and tongues of fire settling on their heads. After this they find themselves suddenly able to speak of 'the wonderful works of God' in any of the languages on earth. This (the effective birth of the Christian church) is commemorated at the feast of Whitsun.

Do you think the 'power' (lines 75-77) in this poem is connected in any way with the story from the Bible? If so, how? If not, what exactly is the 'power' referred to in the poem? What kind of 'being changed' has produced it?

Language practice – structures

15 Pick out all the words or phrases relating to time including times of day and dates, as well as conjunctions and adverbs such as *when, later,* etc) from 'Adlestrop' and 'The Whitsun Weddings'. Next to each write the line number where it occurs. You should find ten.

(Note: check your answers in the Key before going on.)

16 Complete these sentences using words from the list in question 15.

a) The poem describes a train stopping at a small country station _____ hot June afternoon.

b) The poet watches and listens _____ a minute, _____ _____ the train leaves.

c) _____ _____ he hears only steam hissing, and someone clearing his throat.

d) _____ he listens, he notices a blackbird singing.

e) The poem describes a journey made _____ Whitsun.

f) Much of what is seen through the windows is desolate, but _____ _____ _____ something beautiful or interesting appears.

g) Couples continue to board the train _____ it is only an hour from London.

h) _____ _____ they have passed several stations does the poet begin to pay attention to the wedding parties.

i) The newly-married couples climb aboard _____ their families and friends wave from the platforms.

j) _____ the poet notices the wedding parties, it seems he cannot stop thinking about them.

17 Fill in the blanks in the following passage about Edward Thomas, using these words (some may be used more than once).

earlier, for, while, until, over, when, by, during, all, at, before, after, today, in, from, to.

Edward Thomas was born of a middle-class London family _____ (a) 1878. He spent most of his childhood in South London, but _____ (b) the school holidays he visited relatives in Wiltshire and Wales. ____(c) staying in Wiltshire, he met a local peasant and poacher, David Uzell, who taught him much about rural traditions, and remained a friend _____ (d) his life. Thomas began to write (he had kept diaries and notebooks) even _____ (e) he went to St Paul's School _____ (f) the age of 13. At St Paul's he met James Ashcroft Noble, a journalist who encouraged him and found publishers for his work _____ (g) the next few years, ____ (h) Noble died _____ (i) 1896. _____ (j) the time Thomas was 18, he had already published a book, *The Woodland Life*, and several articles.

Thomas studied history at Lincoln College, Oxford, but _____ (k) he was still a student his lover, Noble's daughter Helen, became pregnant. They married shortly _____ (l). In June 1900, Thomas graduated, but the birth of his son six months _____ (m) was a distraction from his studies and he gained only a Second Class Degree.

_____ (n) Oxford, he moved back to London and decided to make a living as a writer. This he did _____ (o) the next 14 years, producing nearly thirty prose books (mainly of topography and biography) and more than a million words of journalism. In spite of his hard work, he struggled constantly for money. His prose books were only mildly successful, and are little admired even _____ (p). It was through his friendship with the American poet Robert Frost (whom he met _____ (q) 1913) that Thomas turned to poetry. _____ (r) December 1914 _____ (s) April 1917, _____ (t) he was killed at the Battle of Passchendaele,

Thomas produced a remarkable series of poems, and it is on these, not his prose books, that his reputation as one of the great poets of the century rests.

18 Now do the same with this paragraph from Philip Larkin's recollection of his early days as a librarian. These are the words that fill the gaps. Some may be used more than once.

before, time, every, to, early on, in time, in, then, after, at, when, at first.

My day began with collecting the day's papers and journals and setting them out in the reading room _____ (a) to open its doors _____ (b) 9 a.m. Then I retreated to the closed lending department and dealt with the post, such as it was, making out applications for inter-library loans and parcelling up volumes to be returned (the post office was, fortunately, directly opposite). From _____ (c) until 3 p.m., _____ (d) the first of the two-hour lending library 'operations' began, my _____ (e) was my own; landladies did not really want to provide fires _____ (f) the morning, and I wrote my novel in the Library _____ (g) taking it back with me to work at after lunch. _____ (h) another session from 6 _____ (i) 8 p.m. I finished reshelving and sorted the issue in time to close the reading room _____ (j) 8.30 p.m. It was a long day, and in some respects a tiring one. Quite _____ (k), I recorded a week when I issued 928 books _____ (l) 20 hours, or 1 about _____ (m) 77 seconds – not much perhaps, but an equal number had to be reshelved, and some of the books could be reached only by ladder. _____ (n) my hand was blistered from stamping books.

(*Philip Larkin*, 'Single-handed and Untrained', in *Required Writing*, London 1983)

19 Write a paragraph describing either a typical working day of yours, or an eventful train journey. Be as precise as possible about times, durations, etc.

Vocabulary

20 Find all the words that describe motion (or absence of motion) in 'The Whitsun Weddings' and write them down.

21 Separate the 'motion' words into the following categories:
   a) verbs that refer to motion upwards or downwards
   b) verbs to do with starting and stopping
   c) verbs referring to attitudes and gestures of the body
   d) verbs that describe slow motion
   e) verbs that describe quick motion
   f) verbs that describe motion in relation to other things

22 Use these words, or others you know, to describe what is happening in these pictures.

Accident at Staplehurst in which Charles Dickens was involved (Illustrated London News)

Railway car at night (Mary Evans Picture Library)

Pullman dining car of the 1870s (Mary Evans Picture Library)

23 Group activity.
  a) Describe one of the pictures above to a partner without saying which one it is. Your partner must guess which picture you are describing.
  b) Choose one of the pictures, but don't tell your partner which one you have chosen. By asking questions about the picture your partner must guess which picture you have chosen.

Extension

24 Read this passage:

In the days when train travel was the norm, we were all rather inclined to take it for granted. After a thirty-year glut of jet and motorway travel, the novelty of which has long since worn off, we can see that train travel was – and when you can get it, still is – comparative bliss. No one who has travelled long distances on a motorway, chained like a dog to his seat, unable to read or drink, blocked by juggernauts from the passing view, deafened by their engines and blackened by their fumes, would wish to repeat the experience for pleasure.

Air travel is little better. One is cramped and disorientated. Chains are *de rigueur* here too; and if you happen to find yourself next to a manic child or compulsive chatterbox, there is little you can do to escape. Airlines attempt to compensate for these deficiencies with piped music, films, and instant alcohol. These overload the system and, combined with a swingeing time-change, lead to total dysfunction; arriving within hours of setting out, one needs two days to recover.

Train journeys, in comparison, have much to offer. Unlike sea or air travel, one has a fair notion where one is; and the countryside, like a moving picture show, unrolls itself before one's eyes. One is transported in comfort, even style, to the wild places of earth – forest, mountain, desert; and always there is the counterpoint between life within the train and life without.

One can move around in a train, visit the buffet for snacks or a drink, play cards (or, on some American trains, the piano), strike up a conversation, read, sleep, snore, make love. Luggage is to hand too, not as in car or airplane, ungetatable in trunk or belly.

Yet the sweetest pleasure of any long train journey lies in its anticipation. I have never eyed any long-distance train I was about to board (except perhaps in Britain) without wondering, as the old hymn says of Heaven,

> What joys await us there?
> What radiancy of glory?
> What bliss beyond compare?

Even if achievement rarely matches promise, one may still day-dream. How green are the vistas, what's for dinner, whom shall I meet? In the end it's the passengers who provide the richest moments of any long-distance trip. For train travel, being constricted both in time and space, magnifies character, intensifies relationships, unites the disparate. Ordinary people become extra-ordinary, larger than life; and in the knowledge that they will not meet again, expansive, confiding, intimate. Let us talk now, you and I: later will be too late.

Ludovic Kennedy *A Book of Train Journeys*, Introduction

What is your opinion about the relative pleasures and pains of travel by rail, air, and road?

Vocabulary

glut: *excess*	swingeing: *huge and forcible*	baggage hold *of aircraft*
worn off: *gone*	the system: *the human nervous*	trunk: *baggage compartment of*
bliss: *extreme happiness*	*system*	*car*
juggernaut: *huge lorry*	dysfunction: *failure to operate*	eyed: *looked at*
de rigueur: (French) *obligatory*	*properly*	disparate: *very different*
manic: *wild and over-active*	a fair notion: *a clear idea*	expansive: *they talk freely and*
chatterbox: *person who talks too*	strike up: *start*	*openly*
much	ungetatable: *you cannot get at*	
piped: *played on the loudspeaker*	*(reach) it*	
system	belly: *(literally, stomach)*	

Beyond the text

25 Compare this poem with 'The Whitsun Weddings' in terms of
   a) the use of a religious festival as the occasion for the poem
   b) the description of England seen through the train windows
   c) the humans beings in the poem
   d) the themes of hope and failure

Man of Sorrows

If ever I meditate Incarnation
I shan't think of the huge thorns
The jumble of horses around the cross
Or a strip of fluttering loincloth;
5 No, I shall think of Trevor.

I met him one Easter afternoon
And had his story as the branch-line
Led us through scrapyard Yorkshire,
Ingrow, Keighley, Shipley, Leeds.
10 Compendium of Nature's off-days:
Weak eyes, beak nose, oily hair
Matted in directionless threads,

A miserly grant of jaw and neck
And forty, living with his dog
15 And an ageing Mother and Dad.
When he left to catch a Shipley bus
To some even more desolate destination

Vocabulary
Man of Sorrows: *the Messiah*
Incarnation: *the Christian belief*
   that God became man in Jesus
thorns, horses, cross,
   loincloth: *typical details from*
   paintings of the crucifixion of
   Jesus
thorns: *the crown of thorns*
   mockingly placed on Jesus's
   head at the crucifixion
jumble: *confusion*
cross: *on which Jesus was killed*
fluttering: *waving in the wind*
loincloth: *cloth to cover the*
   genitals
branch-line: *secondary railway*
   line
scrapyard: *a place where old*
   metal is collected
beak: *the hard exterior of a bird's*
   mouth
matted: *like a mat*
miserly: *mean, ungenerous*
grant: *something given, subsidy*

And two extra days of eventless holiday,
He turned to wave at me three times
20 As if such chances composed friendship;
Then set out belted into anorak
As the wind raged at his ankles
Flogging thin cloth around bone.

I rode on in horror at the sacrifice
25 Of being him: imagine some decree
To exchange one's friends and future
For that stifling, sterile circle!
So I shouldn't think of those things
Irrevocably beautified by art —
30 No, I should think of a man
Held at arm's length by all beauty.

Steve Ellis

eventless: *without events, with nothing happening*
belted into anorak: *wearing a waterproof jacket with a belt*
raged: *blew angrily*
flogging: *whipping*
decree: *command from a supreme authority*
stifling: *suffocating*
sterile: *barren, unable to generate life*
circle: *ie his family and dog*
irrevocably: *in a way that cannot be changed*
at arm's length: *at a comfortable distance*

26 Read this poem and answer the questions.

Not Adlestrop

Not Adlestrop, no – besides, the name
hardly matters. Nor did I languish in June heat.
Simply, I stood, too early, on the empty platform,
and the wrong train came in slowly, surprised,
5   stopped.
Directly facing me, from a window,
a very, *very* pretty girl leaned out.

When I, all instinct,
stared at her, she, all instinct, inclined her head away
10 as if she'd divined the much-married life in me,
or as if she might spot, up platform,
some unlikely familiar.

For my part, under the clock, I continued
my scrutiny with unmitigated pleasure.
15 And she knew it, she certainly knew it, and would
not
glance at me in the silence of not Adlestrop.

Only when the train heaved noisily, only
when it jolted, when it slid away, only *then*,
20 daring and secure, she smiled back at my smile,
and I, daring and secure, waved back at her waving.
And so it was, all the way down the hurrying
platform
as the train gathered atrocious speed
25 towards Oxfordshire or Gloucestershire.

Dannie Abse

Vocabulary
languish: *feel lazy and sleepy*
divined: *guessed*
spot: *see*
familiar: *friend*
scrutiny: *close observation*
unmitigated: *constant*
glance: *look quickly*
heaved: *pulled with an effort*
jolted: *moved suddenly*
atrocious: *horrible.*

a) What is this poem about?
b) Why do you think it is called 'Not Adlestrop'?
c) Having read it, read 'Adlestrop' again. Does 'Not Adlestrop' make you see anything new in Edward Thomas's poem?
d) Say which poem you prefer, and why.

Authors

Edward Thomas (1878-1917): see Question 17

Philip Larkin (1922-85) was born and grew up in Coventry, studied at Oxford University, and worked all his life as a librarian. By general assent the finest poet of post-war Britain, his small output (six slender volumes of verse) proves that quality not quantity is what matters, even today. As well as poetry, he wrote two novels – *Jill* (1946) and *A Girl in Winter* (1947) – and a book about jazz – *All What Jazz* (1970). A book of miscellaneous prose pieces, *Required Writing,* was published in 1983, and his *Collected Poems* in 1988.

Asked once, in an interview, whether his favourite subjects were 'failure and weakness', he replied: 'I think a poet should be judged by what he does with his subjects, not by what his subjects are. Otherwise you're getting near the totalitarian attitude of wanting poems about steel production figures . . . Poetry isn't a kind of paint-spray you use to cover selected objects with. A good poem about failure is a success.'

Dannie Abse was born in Cardiff in 1923, studied medicine and now works as a doctor in London. He has written plays and novels as well as poetry, and two volumes of autobiography: *A Poet in the Family* (1974) and *A Strong Dose of Myself* (1983). His collected poems to date are published under the title *White Coat, Purple Coat* (1989).

Steve Ellis was born in York in 1952, and studied in London. He is a lecturer in English at Birmingham University. He has published a book of literary criticism, *Dante and English Poetry* (1983), and one volume of poems: *Home and Away* (1987).

7 Culture

*The National Gallery
by Stanley Anderson
(Victoria and Albert Museum)*

Before you read

All of the following are part of modern culture or civilization:
*video rental shop   museum of science   betting shop
theatre   arts centre   amusement arcade   public library
circus   discotheque   art gallery   football stadium
film club   striptease club   pub   university
motor racing track   bingo hall   jazz club   funfair
archaeological museum*

1   Divide this set of places into two categories, A and B.

2   Give a name to each category.
    Check your answers in the key before going on.

3   When you have free time, do you generally go to places in
    Category A or Category B, or a mixture of the two?

4   Do you think one category is 'better' than the other in any way?
    Why?

5   Is one category growing at the expense of the other?

6   Read the following poems, and say which of the two types of
    culture each poet seems to prefer.

Seth Compton

When I died, the circulating library
Which I built up for Spoon River,
And managed for the good of inquiring minds,
Was sold at auction on the public square,
5 As if to destroy the last vestige
Of my memory and influence.
For those of you who could not see the virtue
Of knowing Volney's *Ruins* as well as Butler's *Analogy*,
And *Faust* as well as *Evangeline*,
10 Were really the power in the village,
And often you asked me,
'What is the use of knowing the evil in the world?'
I am out of your way now, Spoon River,
Choose your own good and call it good.
15 For I could never make you see
That no one knows what is good
Who knows not what is evil;
And no one knows what is true
Who knows not what is false.

Edgar Lee Masters

> **Vocabulary**
> circulating library: *library which lends books (see Question 15 below)*
> Spoon River: *an imaginary town (see Author Biography on Masters)*
> inquiring minds: *people who want to increase their knowledge and understanding*
> Ruins, Analogy, Faust, Evangeline: *well-known Eighteenth and Nineteenth Century books of history, religion, drama and poetry*
> the power: *the political power*
> I am out of your way now: *I no longer obstruct you*

Hubert's Museum

When I was young and used to wander
down to Times Square on a Saturday
to see a movie with social significance,
eg, *The Battleship Potemkin*,

5 passing Hubert's Museum I'd look at pictures
of Ike and Mike, World Famous Midgets,
and Sahloo Snake Dancer,
and Princess Marie, the Ape with the Human Brain.

Now looking back, it's not the crowd scene
10 on the steps that I remember –
'A marvel', *New Masses*, 'of direction' –
nor the storming of the Winter Palace,

but the body of the Crocodile Man,
and the face of El Fusilado,
15 who 'faced a firing squad, received 8 bullets
through the body and head, yet LIVED!'

Louis Simpson

> **Vocabulary**
> Times Square: *in the centre of New York*
> The Battleship Potemkin: *a film by the Russian director Eisenstein, regarded as one of the most important films of the early twentieth century*
> Sahloo: *the snake-dancer's name*
> the crowd scene, storming of the Winter Palace: *scenes from The Battleship Potemkin*
> New Masses: *a magazine*
> El Fusilado: *(Spanish) the man who has been shot.*

First reaction

7   Would you say that the two poets' ideas of culture are
a) opposed?   b) similar?   c) complementary?

Close reading

Seth Compton

8   Who or what is the subject of the following verbs?
a) 'managed' (line 3)   **b)** 'was sold' (line 4)   **c)** 'were' (line 10)

9   Who is 'you' in line 11?

10 What does Seth Compton imply about books in lines 11-12?
a) that they teach people evil things?
b) that they teach people good things?
c) that they teach people unpleasant things?

11 What is Seth Compton's philosophy as expressed in the last
four lines?
a) 'Good', 'evil', 'true', and 'false' are relative terms which are
absolutely meaningless on their own.
b) Knowledge is essential in forming correct moral and
intellectual judgements.
c) There can be no good without evil, and no truth without
falsehood.

12 Do you think that Seth Compton was popular or unpopular?
Quote from the poem to support your judgement.

Hubert's Museum

13 True, false or partly true?
a) Louis Simpson thinks *Battleship Potemkin* is far more
interesting than Hubert's Museum.
b) Simpson quotes *New Masses* ironically.
c) Hubert's Museum is a museum of natural history.
d) Simpson remembers the pictures from Hubert's Museum
because they frightened him.
e) Simpson cannot remember the crowd scene on the steps in
Battleship Potemkin very clearly.
f) Simpson thinks popular entertainment can be just as
memorable as serious films.

g) Simpson begins 'When I was young' to show how shallow his opinions were in his youth.

h) Simpson proposes 'memorability' as a standard of judgement for culture.

Structure practice

14 Write down all the relative clauses in the two poems (there are six of them).

15 Combine each of the following groups of sentences into one sentence, using relative clauses.

Example:
This is the public library. You can borrow books here. You can also use the reference section to find useful information.

Answer:
This is the public library, where you can borrow books and use the reference section to find useful information.

a) Circulating libraries were popular in Britain for 200 years. The public borrowed books from them for a fee. The libraries stimulated the self-education of the working classes.

b) The first circulating library was set up in Edinburgh in 1726 by Allan Ramsay, a poet and bookseller. His editions of medieval Scottish poetry and ballads contributed to the revival of Scottish vernacular poetry.

c) Eighteenth century circulating libraries were often criticized for popularizing light romantic novels. These were read largely by young women, and were considered improper.

d) One of the most famous Nineteenth century circulating libraries was W H Smith's. Smith's was the predecessor of a well-known chain of stationers, newsagents and booksellers. Its shops can be seen today in towns all over Britain.

e) Another well known library was Boot's. This was set up by the Nottingham businessman Jesse Boot in the late nineteenth century. Customers would ask for suggestions for books from the specially-trained librarians.

f) Circulating libraries remained popular in the 1920s and 1930s. They declined after World War II and had all closed by 1970.

g) The first public libraries were opened in Britain in the 1840s and 1850s. Canterbury was the earliest of them (1847).

h) London's first public library (Westminster) opened in 1857. It did not have a second one until Wandsworth Public Library opened in 1885.

i)   By 1900 there were 400 public libraries in Britain. They were paid for by a small addition to the rates (local taxes). Some people objected to this addition.

j)   The American philanthropist Andrew Carnegie gave enormous sums of money for public libraries in Britain and the USA. He made his fortune from steel manufacturing. His most famous saying is: 'the man who dies rich dies disgraced'.

k)   By 1928 a public libraries service existed in most counties in Britain. This service included children's libraries and village reading rooms.

16 Use the following notes to write a short account of the development of public libraries in the USA. Use relative clauses wherever possible.

First US Library: Harvard University Library Founded 1638. Money and 400 books from John Harvard, a Massachussetts priest.

First free lending libraries founded by Thomas Bray (English priest), late seventeenth century. Interest in libraries waned on Bray's death. (waned: decreased)

First successful public libraries: subscription libraries, founded by Benjamin Franklin and friends in Philadelphia (1731): The Library Company of Philadelphia. Members paid subscription and borrowed books. Original collection still exists.

US Library of Congress (now the world's biggest) built up from Thomas Jefferson's personal library (bought from him 1815).

Ideal of free public education led to growth of public libraries. First public library paid for by taxes founded in Peterborough, New Hampshire, 1833. The idea spread quickly.

1853 first national convention of US librarians (New York).

1876 Melvil Dewey published Dewey Decimal Classification (system of classifying books now in use all over the world).

1881-1919 Andrew Carnegie (steel millionaire) helped to build 1,700 libraries in the USA.

Twentieth century: vast development of libraries and their services.

Vocabulary

17 Number the following words in order from low to high in terms of
   culture using numbers 1-11.

vulgar ___	*crass* ___	*popular* ___
sophisticated ___	*simple* ___	*complex* ___
crude ___	*philistine* ___	*intellectual* ___
moronic ___	*flashy* ___	

18 Use a dictionary to complete the table of derivatives below.
   (Note: where you see the symbol #, no derivative exists.) The
   first one is done for you.

ADJECTIVE	NOUN (person)	NOUN (quality)
vulgar	#	vulgarity
sophisticated		
intellectual		
philistine		
crass	#	
moronic		#
popular	#	
simple		
complex	#	
intelligent	#	
flashy	#	
crude	#	
cheap	#	

19 Look at these pictures and say what you think the reaction of
a) Seth Compton   b) the speaker in 'Hubert's Museum' might be.

Bo Diddley (London Features International)   *Orchestra of the Golden Age*
by Denis Thorpe *(The Guardian)*

Extension

20 Write a short account (200-300 words) of the life of a
philanthropist in your country; or the history of a cultural
institution you admire. (Use a reference book to obtain
information if necessary.)

Beyond the text

Read this poem and answer the questions.

To a Poet a Thousand Years Hence

I who am dead a thousand years
And wrote this crabbed post-classic screed
Transmit it to you – though with doubts
That you possess the skill to read,

5 Who, with your pink, mutated eyes,
Crouched in the radioactive swamp,
Beneath a leaking shelter, scan
These lines beside a flickering lamp;

Or in some plastic paradise
10 Of pointless gadgets, if you dwell,
And finding all your wants supplied
Do not suspect it may be Hell.

But does our art of words survive –
Do bards within that swamp rehearse
15 Tales of the twentieth century,
Nostalgic, in rude epic verse?

Or do computers churn it out –
In lieu of songs of War and Love,
Neat slogans by the State endorsed
20 And prayers to *Them*, who sit above?

How shall we conquer? – all our pride
Fades like a summer sunset's glow:
Who will read me when I am gone –
For who reads Elroy Flecker now?

25 Unless, dear poet, you were born,
Like me, a deal behind your time,
There is no reason you should read,
And much less understand, this rhyme.

John Heath-Stubbs

Vocabulary
crabbed: *difficult, irritable*
screed: *piece of writing*
transmit: *communicate*
mutated: *genetically altered*
crouched: *bent low*
scan: *read*
flickering: *shining unsteadily*
pointless: *without purpose*
dwell: *live*
wants: *needs*
bards: *poets (archaic)*
rehearse: *tell*
rude: *crude, rough*
churn out: *produce mechanically*
in lieu: *instead*
slogans: *political or advertising phrases*
endorsed: *approved*
Elroy Flecker (1884-1915): *a diplomat and poet who wrote much about the Orient (and is little read now)*
a deal: *much*
behind your time: *in the wrong age (too late)*

21 In stanzas 2-3, the poet gives two possible versions of the future.
   a) What are they?
   b) What will decide which of these versions is true?

22 In stanzas 4-5, the poet gives two possible versions of poetry in the future. Briefly, how would you describe these in your own words?

23 In line 21 ('How shall we conquer?')
   a) Who are 'we'?
   b) What kind of conquest is the poet thinking of?

24 Which of the following summaries is closest in meaning to stanza 7?
   a) Only poets who are behind their time can understand this poem.
   b) The best poets are those who are behind their time.
   c) No-one will be able to understand this poem.

25 This vision of the future, like most others in literature, is clearly based on the present, on which it is also a comment. What do you think is the vision of the present implied by this poem? Do you agree with it? Say why.

26 What similarities can you find between this poem and 'Seth Compton' or 'Hubert's Museum?'

Authors

Edgar Lee Masters (1869-1950) was born in Kansas and grew up in southern Illinois. He worked as a lawyer in Chicago. He wrote nearly fifty books of poetry and fiction, but his most famous work was *Spoon River Anthology* (1915), a series of poetic epitaphs on the inhabitants of an imaginary town through several generations.

Louis Simpson was born in Jamaica in 1923 and was educated at Columbia University. He has worked in publishing and taught at Berkeley and the State University of New York, where he is now Professor of English. He has published more than a dozen volumes of verse (including *At the End of the Open Road,* which won the Pulitzer Prize in 1964), a novel, an autobiography (*Air with Armed Men,* 1972) and two studies of modern poetry (*Three on the Tower,* 1975, and *A Revolution in Taste,* 1979). 'I aim at transparency,' he has said, 'to let the action, feeling, and idea come through with no interference.' His *Selected Poems* 1949-83 were published under the title *People Live Here* (New York, 1983).

John Heath-Stubbs was born in London in 1918, and was educated at Oxford University. He has taught at Alexandria, Leeds and Michigan Universities, and published books of literary criticism and plays as well as nineteen volumes of poetry. He has edited selections of poems by Pope, Gray, Swift, Shelley and Tennyson, and translated Leopardi, Hafiz, de Vigny and *The Ruba'iyat of Omar Khayyam.* His *Collected Poems 1943-87* was published in 1988.

8 Satire

Man of the House: Hausherr
by George Grosz

'The employment, in speaking or writing, of sarcasm, irony, ridicule, etc in denouncing, exposing, or deriding vice, folly, abuses, or evils of any kind'

(*Oxford English Dictionary*, 1933)

'The satirist is a kind of self-appointed guardian of standards, ideals and truth . . . who takes it upon himself to correct, censure, and ridicule the follies and vices of society and thus to bring contempt and derision upon aberrations from a desirable and civilized norm.'

(J A Cuddon, *A Dictionary of Literary Terms*, 1979)

'Satire is a sort of glass wherein beholders do generally discover everybody's face but their own.'

(Jonathan Swift, Preface to *The Battle of the Books*, 1704)

Before you read

1   Look at the definitions of 'satire' (or 'satirist') above. What do you
    think are the 'follies and vices of society' today? Make a list.

2   Group activity. Compare your list with those of other students.
    Do you agree? Find one you disagree about, and try to persuade
    your partner that he/she is wrong.

3   Traditionally, the Seven Deadly Sins are *Pride, Wrath, Envy,
    Lust, Gluttony, Avarice, Sloth.* Do you think these are still the
    deadliest sins today? Would you add any, or take any away?

4   Read this poem and decide which folly or vice the poet is
    ridiculing:

Agony Calories

The cooling seaward echo of his screams
Locked in the flesh:

Succulent beyond dream, a live-boiled lobster,
Terror-fresh!

5   How much pain can you eat?

But wait –
Given a choice in the matter,
Our friend Mr Lobster
Would very much rather
10 You didn't plunge him *straight*
Into a pan of boiling seawater
(You knew that by the noise)
But *simmered* him to a *gradual* death
At eighty-five degrees, a method
15 Mr Lobster *very much enjoys*!

(You can tell by the way he
Bobs about:
Stick a weight on the lid so
He can't pop out!)

20 Now. See how much –
But wait!

On page two hundred and seventy-eight
Of *Fish Cookery* by Jane Grigson –
'How to Cut up Live Lobster'
25 So the lobster doesn't cut up! He'll love it.
No fooling with boiling and cooling. Just
Winkle out the place

Vocabulary
calorie: *unit expressing the
energy-value of foods*
The cooling . . . flesh *(lines
1-2): the lobster's screams for its
home (the sea) are preserved in
its flesh after it is cooked*
succulent: *delicious to eat*
beyond dream: *better than a
dream*
live-boiled: *boiled while still
alive*
terror-fresh: *a parody of slogans
used in food-packaging – 'farm
fresh', 'dairy fresh', etc.*
plunge: *push quickly into water*
simmer: *boil gently*
bob: *move up and down*
stick: *(colloquial) put*
pop: *(colloquial) jump*
cut up: *cut up into pieces;
(colloquial) get angry*
fooling: *(colloquial) wasting
time and effort*
winkle out: *find in a hidden
place*

Lobster
by Taurus Graphics

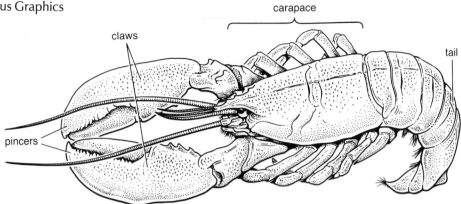

claws

carapace

tail

pincers

Where the tail joins up with the carapace
And whack it with a cleaver. Smash him in half!

30 *You'll* get a thrill –
And you'll hear Mr Lobster laughing,
You'll hear Mr Lobster laughing,
Yes, you'll hear Mr Lobster laughing
All the way to the grill!

35 Cut off the claws and crack them.
Crosscut the tail into slices.
Stack them.
Likewise, *lengthwise*
Split the head: then
40 Mr Lobster
Must be dead! It's

Alla marinara,
A l'américaine
Courchamps,
45 *Bonnefoy,*
A
La
Crême.

A la mayonnaise . . .
50 *A la Charentaise . . .*
Newburg!
        A l'aurore!
A l'anise!
        THERMIDOR!

55 Consume the entire insides of the arthropod
Except for the black
Intestinal canal and the sac
Of grit. Savour

carapace: *(zoology) shell*
whack: *(colloquial) hit very hard*
cleaver: *meat axe*
thrill: *excitement*
alla marinara . . .
    THERMIDOR!: *recipes for*
    cooking lobster
arthropod: *(zoology) animal*
    with jointed feet (Insects,
    Spiders, Crustacea, etc
sac: *(anatomy) small bag or*
    pouch in the body
grit: *tiny pieces of stone*
savour: *taste with pleasure*

Every bit. Then
60   leaning well back
In your rockpool,
              letting
The slurrying sucked salt and the
                      plankton pick
65 Your mandibles clean,
                  between
The pincers of your
              bigger but niftier
        LEFT
70   CLAW

Nip off the tip of the huge cigar!
Ignite delight in the gloom
Of your basement home: a treat to tell
Time by the barnacles
75 Squeezing your shell
As over the flame you wait for the pungent
Pain to bunch and mass:
It's a natural state: it's only

Natural Mr Lobster
80 And natural gas.

                    Kit Wright

rockpool: *pool among rocks left by the tide, where crustacea (small crabs, crayfish etc) are often found*
slurrying: *muddy and sloppy*
plankton: *microscopic marine animals*
mandibles: *(anatomy/zoology) jaws*
pincers: *tool or limb for gripping (eg at the end of a lobster's claw)*
niftier: *(colloquial) more agile, better*
nip: *cut*
ignite: *light*
gloom: *depressing or melancholy darkness*
basement: *rooms in a building below ground-level*
treat: *special pleasure*
barnacles: *tiny shellfish that stick to boats, crustacea, rocks, etc*
pungent: *sharp (in taste or smell)*
bunch: *collect together*
mass: *gather into one piece*
natural gas: *(1) gas found under the earth, used for cooking and heating; (2) gas produced in the intestines*

First reaction

5   Why do you think the poem is called 'Agony Calories'?
    a)   The calories come from the lobster's agony.
    b)   The calories in the lobster cause agony to the eater.
    c)   Both of these.

Close reading

6   Look at this definition of *irony*:
    'The two basic kinds of irony are verbal and irony of situation
    . . . At its simplest, verbal irony involves saying what one
    does not mean. Johnson defined it as a mode of speech in
    which the meaning is contrary to the words . . . Situational
    irony occurs when, for instance, a man is laughing uproariously
    at the misfortune of another even while the same misfortune,
    unbeknownst, is happening to him.'
                    (J A Cuddon, *A Dictionary of Literary Terms*)

There are many examples of verbal irony in this poem. An obvious one is: 'a method/Mr Lobster *very much enjoys*'. Can you find some more examples of verbal irony in the poem?

7 Between lines 60 and 77, the person who eats the lobster is addressed as if he has now *become* a lobster. The first sign of this is the word 'rockpool' (line 61). What other signs are there?

8 In what way is the transformation of the eater into a lobster an example of 'irony of situation'?

9 What do you think is the main idea behind this poem?
   a) killing animals for food is wrong.
   b) there is something sadistic in the way we cook lobster.
   c) there is something sadistic in all human pleasure.
   d) nature takes revenge on us for our cruelty.

10 Read this poem by John Betjeman, and decide what vices or follies are being ridiculed here:

In Westminster Abbey

Let me take this other glove off
  As the *vox humana* swells,
And the beauteous fields of Eden
  Bask beneath the Abbey bells.
5 Here, where England's statesmen lie,
  Listen to a lady's cry.

Gracious Lord, oh bomb the Germans.
  Spare their women for Thy Sake,
And if that is not too easy
10   We will pardon Thy Mistake.
But, gracious Lord, whate'er shall be,
  Don't let anyone bomb me.

Keep our Empire undismembered,
  Guide our Forces by Thy Hand,
15 Gallant blacks from far Jamaica,
  Honduras and Togoland;
Protect them Lord in all their fights,
  And, even more, protect the whites.

Think of what our Nation stands for,
20   Books from Boots' and country lanes,
Free speech, free passes, class distinction,
  Democracy and proper drains.
Lord, put beneath Thy special care
  One-eighty-nine Cadogan Square.

Vocabulary
Westminster Abbey: *the most famous church in London*
vox humana: *a 'stop' (making a sound like a voice) on a church organ*
swells: *grows louder*
beauteous:*(archaic) beautiful*
Eden: *England, which the speaker thinks of as a paradise. In a famous patriotic speech in* Shakespeare's **Richard II**, *England is described as 'This other Eden, demi-paradise' (II,i, 42).*
bask: *lie in the sun*
lie: *are buried*
Germans: *the enemy in World War II*
spare: *do not kill*
for Thy Sake: *a standard phrase from Church prayers, meaning 'for Your [God's] Honour' (the capital letters are customary in references to God)*
whate'er: *(archaic) whatever*
undismembered: *a pompous way of saying 'complete'*
Forces: *armed forces*
gallant: *brave*
stands for: *signifies*
Boots': *a large circulating library (see Chapter 7, 'Culture', Question 15e)*
free passes: *free tickets on public transport for the armed forces*
189 Cadogan Square: *the speaker's home, in one of the richest areas of London*

₂₅ Although dear Lord I am a sinner,
　　I have done no major crime;
　Now I'll come to Evening Service
　　Whensoever I have the time.
　So, Lord, reserve for me a crown,
₃₀ And do not let my shares go down.

　I will labour for Thy Kingdom,
　　Help our lads to win the war,
　Send white feathers to the cowards,
　　Join the Women's Army Corps,
₃₅ Then wash the Steps around Thy Throne
　In the Eternal Safety Zone.

　Now I feel a little better,
　　What a treat to hear Thy Word,
　Where the bones of leading statesmen
₄₀　　Have so often been interr'd.
　And now, dear Lord, I cannot wait
　Because I have a luncheon date.

John Betjeman

Service: *meeting for worship and prayer*
crown: *place in heaven*
shares: *investments on the Stock Exchange*
white feathers: *these were handed to young men not in military uniform during both World Wars as a symbol of cowardice*
Women's Army Corps: *Women's section of the army*
Throne: *king's ceremonial seat*
Safety Zone: *area in which you are safe from bombs, falling buildings, etc*
treat: *special pleasure*
interr'd: *buried*

First reaction

11 Look at these photographs of British women in the 1940s. Which do you think is most like the speaker of this poem? Why?

(Hulton-Deutsch Collection)

(Hulton-Deutsch Collection)

(Hulton-Deutsch Collection)

Close reading

12 'Gracious Lord, oh bomb the Germans'. (line 7)

There is a contradiction in this line, which reveals that the person speaking does not think carefully about the words she uses. What is the contradiction?

13 a) Having requested God to bomb the Germans, the lady goes on, in stanzas 2-4, to ask for protection for seven things. What are they?

b) Some of the things she wants protected are clearly more important to her than others. Can you place them in order of priority?

most important to her

1 _____

2 _____

3 _____

4 _____

5 _____

6 _____

7 _____

least important to her

14 The lady then promises to do certain things in return for God's protection, but adds two further requests (stanzas 5-6). What are these requests? Where would you place them on her scale of priorities (13b above)?

15 There are two separate lines where the lady reveals that her social life is more important to her than religion. Which are they?

16 'Think of what our Nation stands for' (line 19) – What does the list that follows (lines 20-22) suggest about the lady's political beliefs?
a) She is a communist.
b) She is a socialist.
c) She is a conservative.
d) She is a fascist.

17 One of Betjeman's most skilful techniques in this poem is his sudden changes of style – especially from the dignified language of traditional prayer (see Question 23 below) to the banal colloquialisms of everyday conversation. A striking example of this is

So, Lord, reserve for me a crown,
And do not let my shares go down.

Another example, where the lapse is from a high-sounding political ideal to something much more earthy, is the line

Democracy and proper drains.

(Of course, one might observe that proper drains are important for public health, but it is the juxtaposition with 'democracy' that gives the effect of absurdity.) This technique is known as *bathos* or *anticlimax*. It was defined by Samuel Johnson as a 'sentence in which the last part expresses something lower than the first', although it is often the style or vocabulary just as much as the subject that produces the bathetic effect.

To check your understanding of this idea, write next to the following lines whether they are examples of anticlimax or not:

Yes or No?

a) Let me take this other glove off
      As the vox humana swells,   _____

b) But gracious Lord, whate'er shall be,
      Don't let anyone bomb me.   _____

c) Gallant blacks from far Jamaica,
      Honduras and Togoland;   _____

d) Lord, put beneath Thy special care
      One-eighty-nine Cadogan Square.   _____

e) Although dear Lord I am a sinner
      I have done no major crime,   _____

f) Now I'll come to Evening Service
      Whensoever I have the time.   _____

g) And now, dear Lord, I cannot wait
      Because I have a luncheon date.   _____

18 Find evidence in the poem to support (or refute) the following judgements of the lady speaking in Betjeman's poem:
a) She is entirely selfish.
b) She is rather stupid.
c) She is a snob.
d) She is a racist.
e) She is complacent.
f) She is a hypocrite.
g) She is very rich.
h) She is strangely likeable.

Language practice – structures

19 'You knew that by the noise'

'You can tell by the way he bobs about' ('Agony Calories', lines 12, 16-17)

Answer these questions using similar structures with *can tell* or *know*:
(For grammatical analysis, see the Key.)

a) How can you tell from the first five lines of 'Agony Calories' that the poet feels pity for lobsters?
b) How do you know that the eater in the poem is turning into a lobster?
c) How can you tell that the lady in Westminster Abbey is wealthy?
d) How do we know that 'In Westminster Abbey' is set in a time of war?
e) How do we know that the lady is conservative in her opinions?
f) How can you tell that she feels superior to black people?
g) How can you tell that she thinks principally of her own convenience and safety?

20 Another way of stating an interpretation is to say *This means . . .* or *This shows . . .* If you are less certain about the interpretation, you can say *This suggests . . .* or even *This seems to suggest . . .*

In the following exercise, phrases are quoted from the poems, and you are invited to interpret them, using *mean/show/suggest/ seem to suggest*. The first one is done for you.

a) 'Mr Lobster'

Possible answer: This suggests that the poet wants us to think of the lobster as a creature with human feelings.

b) 'On page two hundred and seventy-eight
Of *Fish Cookery* by Jane Grigson'
c) 'Smash him in half!'
d) 'the huge cigar'
e) 'Spare their women'
f) 'class distinction'
g) 'Send white feathers to the cowards'
h) 'What a treat to hear
Thy Word Where the bones of leading statesmen
Have so often been interr'd.'

Language practice – vocabulary

21 Read Passage A about preparing and cooking lobsters, then fill in the gaps in Passage B with the verbs given below it:

Passage A
'Put the lobster into the cold water, and bring it up to simmering point: weight the lid to stop the lobster jumping out. This method is recommended by the RSPCA [Royal Society for the Prevention of Cruelty to Animals] as being painless – the lobster gets dopier as the temperature rises, and expires quietly at 80°F. When simmering point is reached, allow 15 minutes for the first pound, and 10 minutes for each pound after that. Remove the lobster, put it on a dish and allow it to cool in the larder.'
'How to cut up live lobster:
   This is essential if you are using live lobster for a fine dish of *Homard à l'américaine*, or *Lobster Newburg*, as it saves you the prolonged business of boiling and cooling. It will also taste better.
   The thing is to kill the lobster instantly. To do this, place a cleaver across the join between carapace and tail and hammer it down with one hard blow. Cut off the claws, and crack them. Cut the tail across into slices, following the joints. Split the head lengthwise and discard the sac of grit and the black intestinal canal and gills. Put coral and lobster liquor and the creamy part, which is the liver or tomally, into a separate bowl for the final stages of the sauce.'

Passage B
'ON _____ (a) WITH LIVE LOBSTERS:

A number of the best French lobster recipes, _____ (b) *homard à l'américaine* and *bisque de homard*, call for the _____ (c) of cut-up raw lobster. This _____ (d) you must buy live lobster and either have it _____ (e) up for you and _____ (f) it immediately, or _____ (g) the cutting yourself. The serious cook really must _____ (h) the task personally. We _____ (i) the following method. _____ (j) very hot water into a large pan or bowl. _____ (k) the lobster under side up on your cutting board; _____ (l) head and claws with a folded towel, _____ (m) lobster firmly down against the board with your left hand. _____ (n) a sharp knife or lobster shears, _____ (o) straight down ½ inch into the belly of the lobster, at the point where tail and chest _____ (p), thus severing the spinal cord and _____ (q) the lobster instantly. Then, to paralyse all muscle spasms, _____ (r) the lobster head first into the very hot water for 5 minutes or until lobster is limp. _____ (s) from water and _____ (t) as directed.'

Verbs
suggest   cut   killing   run   do   place   cook   covering
plunge   hold   remove   using   means   sautéing   cut   including
join   dealing   cut   face up to

22 One of the two passages above comes from *Fish Cookery* by Jane Grigson, which is quoted in Kit Wright's poem. Which passage is it: A or B?

Compare the passage to the poem. What changes has the poet made to the passage?

23 The two prayers below come from *The Book of Common Prayer* which was written in the sixteenth century and used for over 400 years by the Church of England. Read through them, and say

  a) which is more similar in content to 'In Westminster Abbey'.

  b) which words and phrases remind you of the poem.

(Note: *thou* and *thee* are archaic forms of *you*. *Thy* is an archaic form of *your*.)

> 'Almighty and most merciful Father; We have erred, and strayed from thy ways like lost sheep. We have followed too much the devices and desires of our own hearts. We have offended against thy holy laws. We have left undone those things which we ought to have done; And we have done those things which we ought not to have done; And there is no health in us. But thou, O Lord, have mercy upon us, miserable offenders. Spare thou them, O God, which confess their faults. Restore thou them that are penitent; According to thy promises declared unto mankind in Christ Jesu our Lord. And grant, O most merciful Father, for his sake; That we may hereafter live a godly, righteous, and sober life, To the glory of thy holy Name. Amen.'

> 'O Lord our heavenly Father, high and mighty, King of kings, Lord of lords, the only Ruler of princes, who dost from thy throne behold all the dwellers upon earth; Most heartily we beseech thee with thy favour to behold our most gracious Sovereign Lady, Queen Elizabeth; and so replenish her with the grace of thy Holy Spirit, that she may alway incline to thy will, and walk in thy way: Endue her plenteously with heavenly gifts; grant her in health and wealth long to live; strengthen her that she may vanquish and overcome all her enemies; and finally, after this life, she may attain everlasting joy and felicity; through Jesus Christ our Lord. Amen.' ('A prayer for the Queen's majesty'.)

Extension

24 Write a defence of: either the lady in Betjeman's poem or the methods of cooking lobster as satirized in Kit Wright's poem.

25 Describe an example from your own experience of some form of vicious, selfish or ridiculous behaviour which you would enjoy seeing satirized.

Beyond the text

26 Read this poem by D H Lawrence, and say briefly
  a) what 'vice, folly, abuse, or evil' Lawrence is attacking here.
  b) whether you think this poem is a satire or not (and say why).
  c) whether you think it more or less effective than the other
    poems in this chapter.

Money-Madness

Money is our madness, our vast collective madness.

And of course, if the multitude is mad
the individual carries his own grain of insanity around
    with him.

5 I doubt if any man living hands out a pound note
        without a pang;
and a real tremor, if he hands out a ten-pound note.

We quail, money makes us quail.
It has got us down, we grovel before it in strange terror.
10 And no wonder, for money has a fearful cruel power
        among men.

But it is not money we are so terrified of,
it is the collective money-madness of mankind.
For mankind says with one voice: How much is he
15   worth?
Has he no money? Then let him eat dirt, and go cold. –
And if I have no money, they will give me a little bread
so I do not die,
but they will make me eat dirt with it.
20 I shall have to eat dirt, I shall have to eat dirt
If I have no money.

It is that that I am frightened of.
And that fear can become a delirium.
It is fear of my money-mad fellow-men.

25 We must have some money
to save us from eating dirt.

And this is all wrong.

Bread should be free,
shelter should be free,
30 fire should be free
to all and anybody, all and anybody, all over the world.

> **Vocabulary**
> pang: *sharp pain*
> quail: *lose courage*
> grovel: *lie face down on the*
>   *ground; behave in a servile*
>   *manner*
> delirium: *frenzied, incoherent*
>   *state of mind*

We must regain our sanity about money
before we start killing one another about it.
It's one thing or the other.

D H Lawrence

Authors

Kit Wright was born in Kent in 1944, and studied at
Oxford. He spent some years teaching, first at a
school in London, then at Brock University, Ontario,
before working as Education Secretary at the Poetry
Society in London (1970-75). He spends much of his
time now touring schools in Britain, giving readings of
his poems. He has published ten books of poetry (half
of them for children). His most recent adult works are
in *Poems 1974-83* and *Short Afternoons* (1989). His
poetry is noted for its wit, clarity, varied use of
metrical forms (including songs), and comedy —
darkened by moments of great intensity.

John Betjeman (1906-84) was born and grew up in
London and studied at Oxford. He was a schoolteacher for a time, then began writing for the
Architectural Review. He edited and/or wrote several
Shell Guides to the counties of Britain, and his poetry
is full of affectionate (sometimes scathing) portraits of
places. Much of his verse is comic, and almost all of it
celebratory. While achieving wide popular acclaim,
he was neglected or looked down on by serious critics
in the 1950s and 1960s, but has now come to be
appreciated even by these for his deceptive poetic
skill, his truth to life, and his ability to capture moods,
memories, nuances, tones of voice, people, land-
scapes and towns with unique precision and subtlety.
He is one of the few poets to have used television as
an effective medium of expression, and his recordings
of his poems are a great delight. He wrote a verse
autobiography in three volumes: *Summoned By Bells*,
High and Low, and *A Nip in the Air*. He was Poet
Laureate from 1972 to 1984.

D H Lawrence (1885-1930) is better-known as the
author of novels such as *Sons and Lovers, Women in
Love*, and *Lady Chatterley's Lover* than as a poet. His
father was a coal-miner in Nottinghamshire, his

mother a teacher; though poor, he managed, by winning scholarships, to stay at school until he was 15, then studied at Nottingham University to be a schoolteacher. He taught for two years in Croydon, but was forced by ill-health to give up. In 1912 he eloped to Germany with his ex-professor's wife, and from then until his death from tuberculosis in 1930 led a wandering life, staying for varying periods in Cornwall, Italy, Ceylon, Australia, the USA, Mexico and France. Much of his work was banned for 'obscenity', although it now seems harmless enough. Yet the sixty years since his death have not diminished his ability to shock conventional opinion. He is greatly admired for his travel-writing, short stories, novels and criticism. Many of his poems, written in free verse of great suppleness and power, convey the extraordinary force, courage and originality of his thinking.

9 Cats and Dogs

Rue Mouffetard
by Marc Riboud

'I would rather see the portrait of a dog I know than all the allegorical paintings they can show me in the world.'   (Samuel Johnson)

'The more I see of men, the more I like dogs.'   (Madame Roland)

Before you read

1   How much do you know about cats and dogs? Here are some facts about them. Write against each sentence whether it applies to cats, dogs, or both.
   a)   They are carnivorous animals of the family Canidae.
   b)   Other members of the family are foxes, jackals and wolves.
   c)   They belong to the family Felidae.
   d)   Other members of the family are tigers, lions and leopards.
   e)   They are the most easily tamed of all animals.
   f)   They were first tamed by the Egyptians 3,500 years ago.
   g)   They were first tamed 8,000 to 9,000 years ago.
   h)   They were used in Egypt to protect granaries against rodents.
   i)   They were sacred animals in Egypt, and thousands were mummified.
   j)   The Egyptian god Anubis is depicted with the head of this animal.
   k)   They have long been associated with witchcraft and sorcery.
   l)   Queen Victoria had statues of them erected in palace gardens.
   m)   They are independent in personality, but not adventurous.
   n)   Their hearing and sense of smell are excellent, but they do not distinguish colours well.
   o)   They can run very fast for a long period.
   p)   They can run very fast, but only in short bursts.
   q)   There is a special mechanism in their feet for retracting the claws.
   r)   Along with the camel and the giraffe, these are the only animals that walk and run by moving both legs on the same side at once.
   s)   There are enormous differences in size between the various breeds.
   t)   They have rough, spiny tongues, with which they clean themselves frequently.
   u)   A small, hairless breed which is edible exists in Mexico.
   v)   They frighten enemies by arching their backs, bristling and hissing.
   w)   When the female is in a fertile state she announces the fact by wailing.
   x)   One breed was trained by Swiss monks to find travellers lost in the snow.
   y)   The vertebrae of the spinal column are attached to muscles, not ligaments, making their backs exceptionally elastic.
   z)   They are quite widely bred for economic purposes.

Cats and Geraniums by Clifford Webb

2   Do you prefer cats or dogs? Why?

3   Which do the authors of the following poems seem to prefer?

Max's Verse

(For Doreen and Ruth)
Cats are graceful and delicate
    with secretive natures.
Cats are most clean in their persons,
    beings of great delight,
5 Brave without foolhardiness, servants
    to no man, creatures
Favoured of gods and poets, carousing
    at the crook of night.
Cats are repositories of Wisdom and of Magic.
10   Cats are the philosophers' teachers.
And these things are true of all cats, the Black,
    the Tortoiseshell, the White,
The Marmalade Tom, the Tabby, the subtle
    Siamese of bevelled features.
15 Dogs, on the other hand, *fawn*, and
    should be shot on sight.

John Whitworth

Vocabulary
foolhardiness: *a foolish disregard for danger*
favoured of: *preferred by*
carousing: *wild and noisy merriment (usually while drinking)*
crook: *hidden corner*
repository: *place of storage*
Tortoiseshell: *cat with fur coloured black, orange and cream*
Marmalade: *cat with fur coloured like orange marmalade*
Tom: *male cat*
Tabby: *cat with striped fur*
Siamese: *a cat with short grey/brown fur and blue eyes*
bevelled: *slanting*
fawn: *show affection, usually in a servile way*
on sight: *at the moment of seeing them*

Mort aux Chats

There will be no more cats.
Cats spread infection,
cats pollute the air,
cats consume seven times
5 their own weight in food in a week,
cats were worshipped in
decadent societies (Egypt
and Ancient Rome), the Greeks
had no use for cats. Cats
10 sit down to pee (our scientists
have proved it). The copulation
of cats is harrowing; they
are unbearably fond of the moon.
Perhaps they are all right in
15 their own country but their
traditions are alien to ours.
Cats smell, they can't help it,
you notice it going upstairs.
Cats watch too much television,
20 they can sleep through storms,
they stabbed us in the back
last time. There have never been

any great artists who were cats.
They don't deserve a capital C
25 except at the beginning of a sentence.
I blame my headache and my
plants dying on to cats.
Our district is full of them,
property values are falling.
30 When I dream of God I see
a Massacre of Cats. Why
should they insist on their own
language and religion, who
needs to purr to make his point?
35 Death to all cats! The Rule
of Dogs shall last a thousand years!

Peter Porter

> **Vocabulary**
> pee: *urinate*
> harrowing: *horrible*
> fond of the moon: *they love the moon*
> stabbed: *wounded with a knife*
> property values: *the price of houses*
> purr: *the low rumbling sound made by cats*

First reaction

4   Choose one of the following as a summary of each poem:
   a)   an attack on cats
   b)   an attack on dogs
   c)   a defence and celebration of cats
   d)   a defence and celebration of dogs

5   Do you think either of these poems is anything more than a joke? If either seems to you to make a serious point, can you say what that point is?

Close reading

Mort aux Chats

6   Which interpretation of line 1 do you agree with?
   a)   This is a prediction.
   b)   This is a resolution.
   c)   This is a command.
   d)   This is a threat.
   e)   This is a promise.

7   Peter Porter uses a variety of arguments to support the proposition 'Death to all cats!' How good do you think these arguments are? Do any of them strike you as dishonest?

8   Here are some of the arguments from the poem (a-e), with some objections (1-5). Match the arguments to the objections.

   a)   Cats consume seven times their own weight in food in a week.

b) Cats spread infection.
c) Cats were worshipped in decadent societies.
d) Our district is full of them, property values are falling.
e) Cats watch too much television.

1   This is true of cats, but also of dogs and all other animals.
2   This sounds plausible, but it is in fact untrue, and in any case completely irrelevant.
3   This puts a false interpretation on commonly-observed behaviour.
4   This is completely illogical. The two things are unrelated.
5   This is based on an absurd and unscientific theory of history.

a) __   b) __   c) __   d) __   e) __

9   **a)** Can you find other arguments in the poem to which 1,2,3,4,5 above might be raised as objections?
    b) Why do you think the poet uses so many dishonest arguments in the poem?
    Do the last two lines help to explain this?

10 Are any of these arguments familiar from another context? Which context?

11 Who are 'I' and 'us' in the poem? Is the poet speaking in his own voice or an assumed voice?

Max's Verse

12 Two of the arguments in 'Mort aux Chats' are answered, either completely or in part, by lines in 'Max's Verse'. Which are they, and which are the answering lines? Which version do you agree with?

13 Look again at the types of dishonest argument listed in Question 8 above. Do these describe any of the arguments used in 'Max's Verse'?

14 Another dishonest form of argument is to describe things in emotive language (words with emotional connotations). An example of this is the word 'fawn'. Here is a dictionary definition:

    '1. To show delight or fondness (by wagging the tail, whining, etc) as a dog does. 2 To affect a servile fondness.'

    a) If the poet had used a neutral term such as *show affection* instead of 'fawn', what would the effect have been on the last two lines of the poem?
    b) Can you find any other examples of emotive language in the poem?

15 John Whitworth uses a number of archaisms in his poem:
'most clean'
'persons'
'servants to no man'
'favoured of'
'carousing'
'Wisdom, Magic'   (use of capital letters)
'philosophers'   (old sense of the word)

   a) Why do you think he does this?
   b) How do these archaisms contribute to the sense of shock that comes in the last two lines?

Language practice – structures

16 Pick out all the words and phrases from 'Mort aux Chats' which express disapproval or distaste. To help you, here are some clues:

disease	excess
dirt in the atmosphere	lack of loyalty
corrupt and undisciplined	lack of creative gifts
did not value	lack of distinction
awful	guilt
intolerably	obstinacy
strange	unnecessary
foul odours	kill

17 Use the same words or phrases (adapting where necessary) to write with distaste and disapproval about dogs.

18 Adapt these phrases, or use others you know, to describe the following:
people who throw litter in the streets
snobs
people who drive dangerously
people who jump queues
people who talk too much
people who claim that everything is always better in their country
a town/area/restaurant/shop/car/house that you dislike
someone who was once a friend, but no longer is

19 Group Activity. Ask another member of the group to tell you what irritates him/her, and why. Can you think of any answers or objections to what your partner says? Change roles, and you express your dislikes and irritations. Answer your partner's questions and defend your opinions.

Vocabulary

20 The following words have multiple meanings in English. Look at the way each one is used in the poem, and decide which definition(s) of those given fits the meaning in the poem most closely:

Max's Verse

del·ic·ate /'delɪkət/ *adj* **1** soft or tender when touched; made of sth fine or thin: *as delicate as silk* ○ *a baby's delicate skin.* **2** very carefully made or formed: fine; exquisite: *a delicate mechanism structure, etc* ○ *the delicate beauty of a snowflake.* **3 (a)** easily injured or damaged; fragile: *delicate china* ○ *a delicate plant.* **(b)** becoming ill easily; not strong: *a delicate child, constitution* ○ *She has been in delicate health for some time.* **4 (a)** showing or needing much skill or careful treatment: *the delicate craftsmanship of a fine watch* ○ *a delicate surgical operation, e.g. on sb's eyes* ○ *her delicate playing of the sonata.* **(b)** showing or needing tact and good judgement in human relations; sensitive: *I admired your delicate handling of the situation.* ○ *We're conducting very delicate negotiations.* **5** (of the senses, of instruments) able to detect or show very small changes or differences; sensitive: *a delicate sense of smell\touch* ○ *Only a very delicate thermometer can measure such tiny changes in temperature.* **6 (a)** (of colours) not intense; soft: *a delicate shade of*

pink. **(b)** (of food or its taste) pleasing and not strongly flavoured: *the gentle, delicate flavour of salmon* ○ *Veal is too delicate for a spicy sauce* **(c)** (of smell) pleasing and not strong: *a delicate perfume, fragrance, aroma, etc.* ▷
(Oxford Advanced Learner's Dictionary)

na·ture /'neɪtʃəʳ/ *n* **1** [U] everything that exists in the world independently of human beings, such as earth and rocks, the weather, and plants and animals: *They stopped to admire the beauties of nature.* (=scenery)*Farming on this bad land is a struggle against nature.* **2** [CU]; the qualities which make someone different from others; character: *She has a generous nature\is generous by nature.\It's (in) her nature to be generous.* **3** [S] a type; sort: *ceremonies of a solemn nature* **4 second nature** an action or ability that has become a habit, as if part of one's character: *Speaking French is second nature to him.*
(Longman Active Study Dictionary)

Mort aux Chats

all right *adj, adv* [F. *no comp.*] **1** safe, unharmed, or healthy: *The driver was rather shaken after the accident, but otherwise all right.* **2** *infml* satisfactory but not very good; acceptable; in a satisfactory or acceptable manner or state: *His work is all right (but he could be faster).\ We're doing all right.* **3** allowable; acceptable: *Is it all right if I go now?* **4** also **right** – (in answer to a suggestion, plan, etc) I\we agree; yes: *'Come tomorrow'. 'All right! What time?'* **5** *infml* beyond doubt; certainly: *He's ill all right: he's got pneumonia.* – See ALRIGHT (USAGE) **6 That's\It's all right** (used as a reply when someone thanks you or says they are sorry for something they have done): *'Sorry I'm late.' 'That's all right'.*
(Longman Dictionary of Contemporary English)

help[1]/help/ *v* **1** [1; T *out*] to do something for (someone who needs something done for them); AID; ASSIST: *Please help me; I can't do it alone.\My father helped me (out) with money when I needed it.\Could you help me (to) life this box?\Trade helps the development of industry.* **2** [1;T] to make better: *Crying won't help (you).\It won't help (you) to cry.\Have you got anything to help a cold?* **3** [T + *v-ing*] to avoid; prevent; change; (only in the phrase **can\can't\ couldn't help**): *I couldn't help crying.\I can't help having big feet.\He never does any more work than he can help.\I can't help it.*(=it's not my fault)*You've broken it now,* **it can't be helped.** (=we must accept it) **4** [T *to*] to take for (oneself), esp. dishonestly: *The money was on the table and no one was there so he helped himself (to it).\'Can I have a drink?' 'Help yourself!'* **Help yourself to** *a drink.*
(Longman Active Study Dictionary)

rule /ruːl/ **1** [C] statement of what can, should or must be done in certain circumstances or when playing a game: *The rule is that someone must be on duty at all times.* ○ *the rules of the game* ○ *rules and regulations.* **2** [C usu *sing*] usual practice of habit; normal state of things: *My rule is to get up at seven every day.* ○ *He makes it a rule never to borrow money.* ○ *She made a rule of eating an apple a day.* ○ *Cold winters here are the exception rather than the rule,* ie it is comparatively rare. **3** [U] authority; government: *the rule of law* ○ *majority rule* ○ *a country formerly under French rule* ○ *mob rule,* ie the state that exists when a mob takes control. **4** [C] straight measuring device, often jointed, used by carpenters, etc. **5** [C] (usu straight) line drawn by hand or printed. **6** (idm) **as a (general) rule** (*fml*) in most cases; usually: *As a rule I'm home by six,* bend the rules ◊ BEND[1] **the exception proves the rule** ◊ EXCEPTION. **a rule of thumb** rough practical method of assessing or measuring sth, usu based on past experience rather than on exact measurement, etc (and therefore not completely reliable in every case or in every detail): *As a rule of thumb, you should cook a chicken for 20 minutes for each pound that it weighs.* **rule(s) of the ¹road** rules regulating the movement of vehicles, ships, etc when meeting or passing each other. **work to ¹rule** follow the rules of one's occupation with excessive strictness in order to cause delay, as a form of industrial protest.
(Oxford Advanced Learner's Dictionary)

21 Find the words in 'Max's Verse' that mean the opposite of:
   a) unpleasantness
   b) gross
   c) cowardly
   d) awkward
   e) caution
   f) filthy
   g) expansive
   h) heavy

22 Fill in this table of derivatives (different parts of speech formed from the same word) – eg *beautiful* (adjective), *beauty* (noun), *beautify* (verb): [NB Where you see this symbol #, it means that no derivative exists.]

ADJECTIVE	NOUN (quality/thing)	NOUN (person)	VERB
	infection	#	
			pollute
#			consume
fond		#	#
	tradition		#
			sleep
	storm	#	
great		#	#
		artist	#
	language		#
	religion	#	#
graceful		#	#
delicate		#	#
secretive		#	#
clean			
		person	
	delight	#	
brave		#	
	favour		
		poet	#
	wisdom	#	#
true		#	#
subtle		# #	

23 Use words from the table on page 115 to complete the blanks in this passage:

In the first two lines of his poem, Whitworth speaks of the _____ (a), _____ (b) and _____ (c) of cats. In the third line he mentions their _____ (d). Clearly he is very _____ (e) of them; they are his _____ (f) as well as those of other poets and gods. Yet his _____ (g) in them is not merely subjective: 'these things are true of all cats', as he says. Where he moves away from strict _____ (h) is in claiming that they are _____ (i) (although their association with magic is _____ (j)). One might also take issue with the phrase 'carousing at the crook of the night'; even if this is '_____ (k) licence' (the poet's freedom to 'bend' reality by skilful _____ (l) manipulation), the fact is that when one is trying to _____ (m), the noise of cats calling amorously to each other can be extremely annoying – a point memorably made by Peter Porter.

'Mort aux Chats', apparently a simple diatribe against cats, is a poem of surprising _____ (n). It can be read on at least three levels. First, as an irritable essay (no doubt based on _____ (o) experience) on cats as domestic pets; second, as an expression of the _____ (p) relationship of cats with dogs – the poem is in the form of canine political propaganda, unfairly claiming that they spread _____ (q) diseases, cause air- _____ (r), indulge in massive over- _____ (s) of food, and so on; third, and most impressively, it is a satire on racism and _____ (t) intolerance, with sinister echoes of Nazism in its reference to 'stabbing in the back' and the rule that 'shall last a thousand years'.

Extension

24 Write a short essay or poem in praise of something you like, or attacking something you dislike. (You can use 'Max's Verse' or 'Mort aux Chats' as a model.)

25 Take one of the quotations printed at the beginning of this chapter and write an essay either agreeing or disagreeing with it.

26 Do you prefer cats or dogs? Write a reasoned justification of your preference.

27 Group activity. Find everyone else in the group who agrees with your preference for either cats or dogs. Form a political party, give it a name, and write a short manifesto for it. When your manifesto is ready, hold a debate with the opposition on the motion 'Dogs are a public nuisance and a health hazard, and should be banned from human society'.

Beyond the text

Read this poem.

O Happy Dogs of England

O happy dogs of England
Bark well as well you may
If you lived anywhere else
You would not be so gay.
O happy dogs of England
Bark well at errand boys
If you lived anywhere else
You would not be allowed to make such an infernal noise.

> **Vocabulary**
> as well as you may: *it is understandable for you to do so*
> gay: *happy*
> errand boys: *boys delivering groceries to people's homes*
> infernal: *hellish, horrible*

Stevie Smith

28 What do you think the poet is saying about England in this poem?

29 Do you think dogs are less 'gay' or less free to bark in other countries? How are dogs treated in your country?

30 It has been said that this is a poem about the political right of free speech. Do you agree?

31 Write an imitation of this poem about the favourite animals of your country, and the privileges they enjoy.

Authors

John Whitworth was born in 1945 in India and educated in Edinburgh, then Oxford. He lives in Canterbury, in England, teaching foreign students, writing poetry and reviews. His first book of poems, *Unhistorical Fragments*, won the 1980 Alice Hunt

Bartlett Award, and was praised for its exuberant wit, craftsmanship and vivid accuracy of observation. 'Max's Verse' comes from his second book, *Poor Butterflies*.

Peter Porter was born in 1929 in Brisbane, Australia, where he was educated and worked as a journalist before moving to England in 1951. He worked as a bookseller and advertising copywriter until 1968. He now works full-time as a writer. His early books contain satiric portraits of London in the 1960s; later works probe deeper into moral questions and are rich in allusions to other cultures. His *Collected Poems* were published in 1983.

Stevie Smith (1902-71) lived in North London with an aunt, wrote three novels and eight books of eccentric and intriguing verse with a sharp comic edge. Her *Collected Poems* were published in 1975.

10 City Life

The Forgotten Gorbals
by Bert Hardy
(Hulton-Deutsch Collection)

Before you read

1   What are the advantages of city life? What are its disadvantages? Make a list of each, and say whether you think cities are good places to live in.

2   Answer these questions about the American city of Chicago. Even if you don't know the answers, choose the ones that you think are right.
   a) Which state of the USA is Chicago in?

Texas	Illinois	Massachussetts
California	Arizona	

b) What kind of climate does it have?

tropical	sub-tropical	arctic
mediterranean	temperate	

c) When was the city founded?

1610	1776	1837
1880	1922	

d) How many people live there?

500,000	1 million	3 million
5 million	10 million	

e) Is it

by the sea	in the mountains
in a desert	on a lake?

f) What are its main industries?

metal and food	aircraft	textiles and paper
automobiles	plastics	electronics

g) What are its problems?

poor sanitation	overcrowding	unskilled immigrants
racial tension	unemployment	crime

h) What is it famous for?

cowboys	jazz	gangsters
film studios	horse-racing	space research

i) Do you know anything else about Chicago?

3   Now read this article about Chicago, and check your answers.

Chicago

Chicago is a huge city in northeastern Illinois that ranks as the leading industrial and transportation center of the United States. According to the 1980 census, it was the second largest city in the United States, after New York City. But in 1982, U.S. Bureau of the Census estimates reported that Los Angeles had passed Chicago in population, making Chicago the nation's third largest city.

About 3 million people live in this energetic city along the southwest shore of Lake Michigan. The Chicago area manufactures more fabricated metals and food products than any other urban area in the United States. Trucks and railroad cars carry more goods in and out of Chicago than in and out of any other city in the United States.

The American poet Carl Sandburg called Chicago the 'City of the Big Shoulders'. And the city does do things in a big way. For example,

Chicago has the world's tallest building, largest grain market, biggest post office building and busiest airport.

Chicago also has one of the world's most beautiful lakefronts. Most of it is public parkland, with broad beaches and lawns stretching far along the shoreline. In addition, the city has an excellent symphony orchestra and fascinating museums of art, history, and science. Chicago surprises many of its almost 8 million annual visitors who learn that the city, which was built for business and industry, also has a tradition of beauty and culture.

Throughout its history, Chicago has been known for providing good jobs. Young men from Germany and Ireland came to Chicago to dig a shipping canal soon after Chicago became a city in 1837. During the next 100 years, thousands of European families came to work in Chicago's factories, steel mills, and shipping businesses. By the late 1800s, Chicago had become an industrial and commercial giant.

In 1871, the Great Chicago Fire destroyed much of the city. But Chicagoans rebuilt their city with a daring that made it a center of world architecture. During the 1920s, Chicago gained a reputation for crime and violence that it has never lived down. Yet this was also a creative period in the arts, and the booming industries in Chicago continued to attract new residents to the city.

Since the 1940s, most newcomers to Chicago have been blacks and whites from poor areas of the South; Hispanic families from Mexico, Puerto Rico, and Central America; and Asian families. Many of these people have lacked the skills and education needed for today's jobs. About a fourth of Chicago's people receive some form of public welfare aid. Other problems include a high crime rate in poor neighborhoods, economically troubled city government and school systems, and a loss of business and residents to thriving suburban areas.

Facts in brief

Population: *City* – 3,005,072. *Metropolitan area* – 6,060,387. *Consolidated metropolitan area* – 7,937,326.

Area; 228 sq. mi (591 km^2). *Metropolitan area* – 1,911 sq. mi. (4,949 km^2) *Consolidated metropolitan area* – 5,694 sq. mi. (14,747 km^2).

Climate: *Average temperature* – January, 25°F. (-4°C); July, 75°F (24°C). *Average annual precipitation* (rainfall, melted snow, and other forms of moisture) – 33 in. (84 cm).

Government: Mayor-council. *Terms* – 4 years for the mayor and the 50 council members.

Founded: 1803. Incorporated as a city in 1837.

(Excerpted from the World Book Encyclopedia. © 1990 World Book Inc. By permission of the publisher.)

Did you find anything surprising in the article? If so, what?

4   Read the following poem, written in 1916 by Carl Sandburg:

Chicago

Hog Butcher for the World,
Toolmaker, Stacker of Wheat,
Player with Railroads and the Nation's Freight Handler;
Stormy, husky, brawling
5   City of the Big Shoulders:

They tell me you are wicked and I believe them, for I have seen your
    painted women under the gas lamps luring the farm boys.
And they tell me you are crooked and I answer: Yes, it is true I have
    seen the gunman kill and go free to kill again.
10 And they tell me you are brutal and my reply is: On the faces of women
    and children I have seen the marks of wanton hunger.
And having answered so I turn once more to those who sneer at this my
    city, and I give them back the sneer and say to them:
Come and show me another city with lifted head singing so proud to be
15   alive and coarse and strong and cunning.
Flinging magnetic curses amid the toil of piling job on job, here is a tall
    bold slugger set vivid against the little soft cities;
Fierce as a dog with tongue lapping for action, cunning as a savage
    pitted against the wilderness,
20   Bareheaded,
    Shoveling,
    Wrecking,
    Planning,
    Building, breaking, rebuilding,
25 Under the smoke, dust all over his mouth, laughing with white teeth,
Under the terrible burden of destiny laughing as a young man laughs,
Laughing even as an ignorant fighter laughs who has never lost a
    battle,
Bragging and laughing that under his wrist is the pulse, and under
    his ribs the heart of the people,
        Laughing!
30 Laughing the stormy, husky, brawling laughter of Youth, half-naked,
    sweating, proud to be Hog Butcher, Toolmaker, Stacker of Wheat,
    Player with Railroads and Freight Handler to the Nation.

Carl Sandburg

Vocabulary
hog: *male pig*
toolmaker: *one who makes tools*
stacker: *person who stacks or*
    arranges things in an orderly
    way
freight handler: *person or*
    company that arranges
    transportation of goods
husky: *tough and virile*
brawl: *fight*
lure: *attract (into a trap)*
crooked: *dishonest*

brutal: *(from brute): inhuman*
wanton: *unnecessary*
sneer at: *despise*
coarse: *opposite of fine*
cunning: *clever in gaining*
    advantage
fling: *literally, throw; here it*
    means shout
curses: *bad language*
toil: *hard work*
pile: *put one on top of the other*
slugger: *a boxer with no*
    technique except hitting hard

lapping: *literally, drinking*
    greedily; here it probably means
    greedy
pitted: *fighting*
wreck: *destroy*
burden: *load*
destiny: *events and conditions of*
    a person's life which he does not
    choose; fate
brag: *boast*
wrist: *joint between hand and*
    arm
pulse: *heart-beat*
ribs: *the curved bones of the chest*

5 Which of the following words best represents the poet's attitude to Chicago?

anguish	shame
hope	pride
despair	aggression
dislike	pleasure

6 The opening lines of 'Chicago' describe the city as if it were a person – butcher, toolmaker, etc. This form of description is called *personification*. Personification is a form of metaphor (see page 34). Notice that Sandburg has used personification not only in the form of nouns, but also of verbs (for example 'shoveling'), adjectives and pronouns.

Write down six personifications from the poem in each of the following categories: nouns – adjectives – verbs. In each case an example is given to help you.

NOUNS	ADJECTIVES	VERBS
butcher	husky	brawling

7 Sandburg uses people in another way too. Look again at lines 6 to 11, then answer the questions.
  a) Are these people metaphorical or real?
  b) What is meant by 'painted women'?
  c) Which of these people seem to benefit from being in Chicago?
  d) Can you find any sentences in the article on Chicago which describe similar people or the problems they represent?
  e) If Sandburg's purpose is to praise Chicago, why do you think he describes such people and their problems?

8 Which of the following summaries of the poem is most accurate?
  a) Chicago is a city for the young.
  b) Chicago is a city for the people who enjoy violence.
  c) Chicago is a corrupt and frightening city.
  d) Chicago is a hard but magnificent city.
  e) Chicago is a destructive but lovable city.
  f) Chicago is a city where people fight and laugh a lot.
  g) Chicago, though rightly proud of its industrial success, is too violent and lawless.
  h) Chicago is rich but dangerously ignorant.

9   Read the following poem, written in 1956.

Chicago Poem

I lived here nearly 5 years before I could
      meet the middle western day with anything approaching
Dignity. It's a place that lets you
      understand why the Bible is the way it is:
5 Proud people cannot live here.

The land's too flat. Ugly sullen and big it
      pounds men down past humbleness. They
Stoop at 35 possibly cringing from the heavy and
      terrible sky. In country like this there
10 Can be no God but Jahweh.

In the mills and refineries of its south side Chicago
      passes its natural gas in flames
Bouncing like bunsens from stacks a hundred feet high.
      The stench stabs at your eyeballs.
15 The whole sky green and yellow backdrop for the skeleton
      steel of a bombed-out town.

Remember the movies in grammar school? The goggled men
      doing strong things in
Showers of steel-spark? The dark screen cracking light
20   and the furnace door opening with a
Blast of orange like a sunset? Or an orange?

It was photographed by a fairy, thrilled as a girl, or
      a Nazi who wished there were people
Behind that door (hence the remote beauty) but Sievers,
25   whose old man spent most of his life in there,
Remembers a 'nigger in a red T-shirt pissing into the
      black sand.'

It was 5 years until I could afford to recognize the ferocity.
      Friends helped me. Then I put some
30 Love into my house. Finally I found some quiet lakes
      and a farm where they let me shoot pheasant.

Standing in the boat one night I watched the lake go absolutely
      flat. Smaller than raindrops, and only
Here and there, the feeding rings of fish were visible 100 yards
35   away – and the Blue Gill caught that afternoon
Lifted from its northern lake like a tropical! Jewel at its ear
      Belly gold so bright you'd swear he had a
Light in there . . . colour fading with his life. A small
      green fish . . .

40 All things considered, it's a gentle and undemanding
      planet, even here. Far gentler

Here than any of a dozen other places. The trouble is
    always and only with what we build on top of it.

There's nobody else to blame. You can't fix it and you
45   can't make it go away. It does no good appealing
To some ill-invented Thunderer
    brooding above some unimaginable crag . . .
It's ours. Right down to the last small hinge it
    all depends for its existence
50 Only and utterly upon our sufferance.

Driving back I saw Chicago rising in its gases and I
    knew again that never will the
Man be made to stand against this pitiless, unparalleled
    monstrocity. It
55 Snuffles on the beach of its Great Lake like a
    blind, red rhinoceros.
It's already running us down.

You can't fix it. You can't make it go away.
    I don't know what you're going to do about it,
60 But I know what I'm going to do about it. I'm just
    going to walk away from it. Maybe
A small part of it will die if I'm not around

    feeding it anymore.

Lew Welch

Vocabulary

sullen: *melancholy*
pound: *bang like a hammer*
stoop: *bend (usually from weariness or age)*
cringe: *bend in fear or servility*
Jahweh: *the God of the Old Testament of the Bible, usually considered unforgiving and terrifying*
bounce: *jump up*
bunsen: *small gas-burner producing a single tall flame, commonly used in laboratories*
stacks: *chimneys*
stench: *foul smell*
stabs: *wounds with a knife*
backdrop: *(theatre) a large painted cloth that hangs across the back wall of the stage*

bombed-out: *bombed to destruction*
grammar school: *in the USA, school before high school*
goggled: *wearing goggles (eye protectors)*
steel-spark: *sparks flying when steel is hammered*
blast: *rush of wind*
Nazi: *the reference is to furnaces in Nazi extermination camps*
nigger: *negro (an insulting term)*
pissing: *urinating (the image here is of squalor and poverty, to contrast with the heroic images of the educational film)*
ferocity: *from fierce*
pheasant: *bird of the genus Phasianus*

feeding rings: *created when fish come to the surface to eat*
Blue Gill: *type of fish*
tropical: *tropical fish*
belly: *under-side, stomach*
ill-invented: *foolishly invented*
Thunderer: *one who makes thunder; God*
brood: *sit; or hang; or think (often angrily)*
crag: *mountain*
sufferance: *permission*
unparalleled: *unique, unequalled*
monstrocity: *a deliberate mis-spelling of monstrosity (meaning a monstrous thing) so that it includes the word city. Compare ferocity (line 28), which is spelled correctly*
snuffles: *breathes noisily*

First reaction

10 Look again at the words in Question 5. Which would you choose
to describe Lew Welch's attitude to Chicago?

Close reading

11 The article quotes a line from Sandburg's poem ('City of the Big Shoulders') to introduce the idea that 'the city does do things in a big way'. Can you find a line or phrase in Lew Welch's poem which might be used to introduce these sentences in the article?
    a) About a fourth of Chicago's people receive some form of public welfare aid.
    b) Chicago also has one of the world's most beautiful lakefronts.

12 Write a simple one-line summary of *Chicago Poem* such as the one you chose in Question 8.

13 Here is a more detailed summary of the poem. Next to each sentence, write down the line numbers referred to:
    a) Emotional impact of Chicago   Lines _____
    b) Visual description of the city   Lines _____
    c) Idealized film version of the city   Lines _____
    d) Dismissal of idealized version   Lines _____
    e) Temporary escape from the city   Lines _____
    f) Thoughts while fishing   Lines _____
    g) Return to the city; reaction   Lines _____
    h) Resolution   Lines _____

14 Say whether the following statements are **True** or **False:**
    a) It is the city's industry and pollution that most offends Welch.
    b) He regards the educational films about industry as harmlessly funny.
    c) The films showed black factory workers urinating in the sand.
    d) After five years he came to accept Chicago's ferocity.
    e) He went fishing and hunting, and found the experience spiritually consoling.
    f) He thinks there is something wrong with the planet.
    g) He thinks Chicago's problems are insoluble.
    h) Returning to Chicago, he understands that he cannot live there any more.
    i) He compares the Lake to a blinded rhinoceros.
    j) The idea at the end is that a city feeds on its inhabitants; if they leave the city will die.

15 What do you think is the point of the simile 'like a blind, red rhinoceros'? Why blind? Why red? What is the similarity between the city and a rhinoceros?

Language practice – structures

16 Go through 'Chicago Poem' and pick out all the uses of *can, can't, could.*

17 Find sentences in the poem that are similar in meaning to the following:
  a) It seems that people can't bear the weight of the sky.
  b) When the gases are burned off, you can see vast flames from the chimneys.
  c) No-one can stand the smell.
  d) My friend couldn't remember anything heroic about the steel-mills.
  e) We can't expect God to help us.

18 Re-write the following sentences from the poem, using *can, can't, could* or *couldn't*:
  a) It's a place that lets you understand why the Bible is the way it is.
  b) I found a farm where they let me shoot pheasant.
  c) The feeding rings of fish were visible 100 yards away.
  d) There's nobody else to blame.
  e) It all depends for its existence upon our sufferance.
  f) Never will the man be made to stand against this.
  g) Maybe a small part of it will die if I'm not around.

Vocabulary

19 Look back to the examples of personification that you listed in Question 6. Write definitions or synonyms (using a dictionary if necessary) for each of them. Eg 'brawling': *fighting;* 'butcher': *someone who prepares and sells meat.*

20 To study the effect of some of these personifications, compare them to phrases conveying similar information in the article about Chicago. For example 'Hog Butcher for the World, Toolmaker' corresponds to 'The Chicago area manufactures more fabricated metals and food products than any other urban area in the United States' (paragraph 2).

   What do you notice when you compare the two versions? Here are some words that we might use in a comparison. Look up any that you don't know in a dictionary, then write some sentences comparing the version in the article with the version in the poem. Example: *the article is more factual than the poem.*

Use these words in your sentences:

concise	memorable	scientific
sober	factual	striking
bland	punchy	

21 a) Find the equivalent phrases in the article to

Stacker of Wheat
Player with Railroads and the Nation's Freight Handler

b) Compare the effect of these phrases with their counterparts in the article.

Extension

22 a) Which of the two poems do you think gives a more objective idea of Chicago?
b) Which corresponds more closely to your experience of big cities?
c) Which poem do you prefer? Why?

Beyond the text

Read this poem, written in 1929, and answer the question that follows:

We Die Together

Oh, when I think of the industrial millions, when I see some of them,
a weight comes over me heavier than leaden linings of coffins
and I almost cease to exist, weighed down to extinction
and sunk into a depression that almost blots me out.

5 Then I say to myself: Am I also dead? is that the truth?
Then I know
that with so many dead men in mills
I too am almost dead.
I know the unliving factory-hand, living-dead millions
10 is unliving me, living-dead me,
 I, with them, am living-dead, mechanical at the machine.

And enshrouded in the vast corpse of the industrial millions
embedded in them, I look out on the sunshine of the South.

And though the pomegranate has red flowers outside the window
15 and oleander is hot with perfume under the afternoon sun
and I am 'il Signore' and they love me here,
yet I am a mill-hand in Leeds
and the death of the Black Country is upon me
and I am wrapped in the lead of a coffin-lining, the living death of my
20   fellow men.

                                                    D H Lawrence

---

Vocabulary
leaden: *made of lead*
lining: *the material on the inside*
 of something
coffin: *box for burying the dead*
blot out: *kill, eliminate*
factory-hand: *factory worker*
enshroud: *cover in a shroud*
 (a cloth for covering the dead)

corpse: *dead body*
South: *southern Europe*
pomegranate: *a fruit-tree*
 growing in the Mediterranean
 (Punica Granatum)
oleander: *a Mediterranean*
 shrub with pink or white flowers
 (Nereum Oleander)

il Signore: *(Italian) the Lord*
Leeds: *an industrial city in the*
 north of England
the Black Country: *the*
 industrial counties of northern
 England

---

23 On the evidence of this poem, what do you think Lawrence's
answer would be to the last six lines of 'Chicago Poem'? How do
you think Welch would answer Lawrence?

Authors

Carl Sandburg (1878-1967) was born in Illinois of
Swedish parents. He left school at 13, and worked in
many different labouring jobs, then fought in the
Spanish-American War. He then continued his education, paying his own way, until he found work on
the *Chicago Daily News*. He published *Chicago
Poems* in 1916, then *Cornhuskers* (1918), *Smoke and
Steel* (1920), *Slabs of the Sunburnt West* (1922),
Good Morning America (1928), and a collection of
folk-songs, *The American Songbag* (1927). He wrote
a 6-volume biography of Abraham Lincoln (1926-39),
an epic novel (*Remembrance Rock*, 1948), and an
autobiography, *Always the Young Strangers* (1953).
His *Complete Poems* won a Pulitzer Prize in 1931, as
did his Lincoln biography in 1940.

Lew Welch (1926-71) was born in Phoenix, Arizona, but grew up in California. He studied English and Music at Reed College and later at the University of Chicago. Between 1953 and 1957 he worked in an advertising company in Chicago, then moved to California, where he left his job to concentrate on writing. For the next thirteen years he did a variety of manual jobs (taxi-driving, salmon-farming, working at the San Francisco docks) while writing and giving readings and teaching occasional poetry-writing courses at universities. He also studied Zen Buddhism and was friendly with Beat Generation writers such as Jack Kerouac, Allen Ginsberg and Gary Snyder. (He is portrayed as David Wain in Kerouac's novel *The Big Sur*). He published four books of poetry, as well as his Collected Poems, *Ring of Bone*, which appeared after his death, in 1973. He said of his own work: 'When I write my only concern is accuracy. I try to write accurately from the poise of mind which lets us see that things are exactly what they seem. I never worry about beauty, if it is accurate there is always beauty. I never worry about form, if it is accurate there is always form.'

D H Lawrence – see Author Biography in Chapter 8, Satire.

Key

Note: Questions with subjective answers are not dealt with here. Where answers are given they are not necessarily the only possible answers. If your answers look something like the ones printed below, then you are probably on the right track.

1 Childhood

3 **a)** 'Incendiary'. **b)** 'Children's Song'. **c)** 'Dead Dog'.

4 **a, b, d)** 'Incendiary'. **c, e)** 'Children's Song'. **f)** 'Dead Dog'.

5 Thomas' meaning seems to be that the children's world is much better than the adults'. The lines also suggest that the children's heaven is better, precisely because it is more immediate (not 'remote'), it is physically present in their lives – not an intangible intellectual concept.

6 **a, b, d, f, g, h)** are false. **c** and **e)** are true.

7 **a)** This suggests an unhealthy, unloved, sad child who communicates badly.
   b) This suggests that the child lacks energy and warmth. He is less alive than the fire.
   c) The match / menagerie of tigers (lines 8-11) and the small boy / sky and stars (lines 12-13).
   d) The boy's.
   e) burnt-out, blaze, match, lighting, pipe, kitchen fire, flame-fanged, on fire, stars, heat, warm.
   f) It is primarily emotional warmth – love. This is a different kind of warmth from that suggested in the rest of the poem, except possibly 'kitchen fire' which, as a symbol of the home, suggests both physical and emotional warmth.

8 **a)** *must have* been
   b) *must have* been
   c) *must have* known him
   d) it (or the season) *must have* been
   e) *must have* been big.

9 **a)** *can't have* felt it before
   b) *can't have* felt too bad
   c) *can't have* been very important to him (or very interesting)

d) *can't have* been loved

e) *can't have* occurred after that date

10 a) You probe and pry, *but/yet* you cannot find the centre.
I only stood three feet tall, *yet* I picked it up.

b) *Although* adults crawl on hands and knees, they cannot enter the child's world.
Although adults have a heaven, it is faded and remote.
Although adults listen to children, they can never understand them completely.
Although he called the dog 'my mongrel', he did not own it.
Although the boy did not cry, he still felt pity.
Although the father knew it wasn't his dog he still buried it for him.
Although the dog is said to have a 'grin', it can't have been happy.

c) *Although* the boy was small
Although matches are useful
Although the child was a criminal
Although he is an adult
Although he says the children's world cannot be entered
Although the poem is partly about the sadness of being an adult

d) The boy was small, *yet* he managed to start an enormous fire
Matches are useful, *yet* they can also be used to cause destruction
The child was a criminal, *yet* the poet sees him as a victim of neglect
The poet is an adult, *yet* he writes as if he were a child
He says the children's world cannot be entered, *yet* he seems to enter it quite successfully
The poem is partly about the sadness of being an adult, *yet* it is also a celebration of childhood

11 1 composed/made up; 2 linguistic; 3 and; 4 tradition; 5 words; 6 have; 7 environment/world; 8 certain/several; 9 well; 10 entered/came in; 11 was; 12 tend; 13 more; 14 combined/mixed/joined; 15 recognizable; 16 spoken; 17 English; 18 find/notice; 19 for; 20 each; 21 seen/regarded/thought of; 22 shorter; 23 more; 24 of; 25 as; 26 most; 27 language.

12 a) All the words are Germanic except for *spiked* (from Latin *spica*), but even this sounds Germanic, as it is monosyllabic.

b) There are many more Romance words in this part: 'remember', 'moderate', 'pity', 'ordinary', 'recollection', 'terror'.

13 The reason may be that lines 9-14 are more analytical, whereas lines 1-8 deal more with facts and actions.
The change in vocabulary also reflects a change in point of view,

from the child's immediate vision to the adult's retrospection and contemplation (but note the relapse in line 12).

15 This is debatable, but certainly the following are enjoyed: regular rhythm, rhymes, nonsense, repetition, the presence of animals.

2   Age

1   These are the traditional costumes of the 'Pearlies' – 'Kings and queens' elected by the street traders of London, originally to protect their interests but now devoted to raising money for charity. They both seem to be pleased, but the man looks slightly uncomfortable.

4   Several answers are possible. 'Freedom', 'convention', 'courage', 'individuality' . . .

5   1-12: What I will do.
13-17: What you can do.
18-21: What we must do now.
22-25: A decision to begin my freedom now.

6   Section 2: can – you.
Section 3: must – we.

7   a) or c).

8   Being free; doing all the things listed in lines 1-12.

9   b).

10 A 11, B 4, C 12, D 7, E 3, F 2, G 10, H 9, I 1, J 6, K 8, L 5

17 a) They   b) life before death

18   a) 4,   b) 3,   c) 4 and 3   d) Yes

19 The whole poem is in free verse.

21 This is a difficult and partly personal question, but it is often said that metre and rhyme make a poem more enjoyable to read aloud, more memorable, and more aesthetically and intellectually pleasing. The words that rhyme also gain a slight emphasis, and communicate with each other outside the syntactic structure of the poem. Another effect of regularity can be to create an unfortunate effect of 'patness' – simplistic, facile neatness of expression. Graves daringly runs this risk in his opening stanza, and then brilliantly exploits it in the second with his list of the horrors of age (decrepitude, senility . . .) and the grim humour of the third. This technique of arranging grim ideas in pretty patterns is sometimes called counterpoint. It can be extremely powerful.

22 'Warning' challenges the common idea of old age as a depressing time of life.
or
'Warning' challenges the common idea that old age is depressing.

23 . . . death really is the end of something.
. . . the finality of death.

24 Many possible answers, but here are some samples:
   a) This reminds us that popular culture is often more vivid and memorable than high culture.
   b) This reminds us that humans are often slaves to money.

25 Sonnet for the Class of '58

No longer students and not likely to succeed,
tonight I remember old friends, scattered far,
who wanted so much once, and now need
only a rise of a hundred pounds or a car,
or a holiday abroad without the wife,
or time to read more, or more fun.
Perhaps never, or only when drunk, does life
seem as it once seemed, a war to be won.
The moving and influential things they devised
have all been said and done, it seems, by others.
Some do the very things that they despised
and recognise the enemy as brothers;
and even those who've gained more power or sense
feel sorry when they feel the difference.

26 **a)** Your interpretation of this line depends on what *you* want from life. An average set of wants might be: money, love, happiness, power, influence, recognition . . .
   b) This one is even more personal; assuming that the students were idealistic once, they probably despised things like banking, accountancy, insurance, industry, politics perhaps also teaching, the Church, etc.
   c) The difference is between how they are now and how they were as students.

3 Images

1 **a)** A personal response: the position of the wings shows their length and beauty, and suggests power and grace; the dramatic sky suggests the power of the elements, especially the winds; the patterns in the sky echo the patterns on the wings, suggesting that the gull belongs in the sky, and to some degree masters it; the eggs suggest fertility, and the gull's maternal instinct; the position of the nest suggests wildness, loneliness, and again perhaps mastery over the sea.
  b) Another personal response: no.

2 The first picture is an illustration for a book called *Glory of Life*, and it expresses this concept very clearly and vigorously. The second is from a field-guide to birds, and is intended purely to help the reader recognize a gull when he sees one. There is almost certainly no expressive intention in it.

3 **a)** personal, subjective impressions, imaginative associations, human attributions, comparisons, colour, position in relation to the speaker and other objects.
  b) scientific information, history, dimensions, facts, temperatures, explanations, astronomical information, theories, distances.

4 The poems have this in common with the first picture; that they are personal, artistic interpretations of their subject, which express feelings towards it. The encyclopaedia article and the second picture are both concerned primarily with giving factual information.

5 A chair.

8 **a)** a fan;   **b)** frost on a grass-blade;   **c)** clarity and whiteness

9 **a)** fog;   **b)** a cat;   **c)** delicacy of movement, stillness, silence.

10 **a)** courage, strength, kingship; **b)** timidity, silence, discretion, weakness; **c)** evil, cunning, death; **d)** protection, strength; **e)** industry, manual labour; **f)** fertility, plenty, goodness, nature; it has also been used to symbolize youth about to die (soldiers before a battle).

12 **a)** young men riding, the horses leaping, sparks from their hooves.
  b) clearly he likes it, and wants to communicate his pleasure to the reader; Pound also being a master technician probably wanted to imitate, verbally and metrically, the energy and elegance and noise of the young men riding. It is also a celebration of spring and the energy that flows through all living things in this season.

13 a) Metaphors.
   b) chimneys are compared to soldiers
   dark shapes against light are compared to cutting
   a cloud is compared to gauze, and the moon to a woman's
   loins
   the position of the moon in the sky is compared to the pose of
   an artist's model
   the moon is compared to the Roman Goddess of Love
   c) orderly arrangement of similar shapes
   sharpness
   covering something beautiful or erotic
   artistic (and perhaps erotic) positioning
   erotic appeal.

14 Descriptive/narrative.

15 a); perhaps a touch of **c)**.

16 a) delicate as flower of grass; **b)** it could easily be both;
   c) delicacy

17 a) descriptive/narrative (though the nettles and the shower could
   perhaps be seen as symbols of fertility).
   b) as in question 12, the answer is almost certainly to share an
   intense personal pleasure, combined with a technical aim,
   which in this case is to write a successful poem about a quiet,
   apparently unremarkable country scene.
   c) they are similar in the speaker's declared pleasure in what he
   sees, and in placing this declaration after the main description.
   They are different in that Aldington's speaker seems to mock
   himself slightly, and therefore to be detached from himself.
   The 'I' of Thomas's poem is completely serious and not
   detached from himself.

20 a) I: evening, six o'clock, ends . . . of days, lighting of the lamps
   (evening)
   II: morning, early,
   III: night, light crept up (dawn)
   IV: skies that fade (sunset); four and five and six o'clock;
   evening newspapers.
   b) It seems to cover 48 hours, from 6 o'clock one evening (I) to
   the next morning (II), to the following night and dawn (III), to
   the afternoon and evening of the day after (IV).

21 a) they are plentiful and obvious: vacant lots, broken blinds,
   lonely cab-horse, muddy feet, dingy shades, furnished rooms
   b) most of the adjectives suggest squalor, weariness, dilapidation
   c) this suggests the generality and repetitiveness of what is being
   described
   d) generally rather depressing.

22 All are possible, though c) is rather unlikely.

23 Line 27 is definition 5; Line 49 is definition 5 too, but perhaps also 4 and 6.

24 This is up to the reader to decide. The lack of names probably indicates that they could be anybody; in other words that they are symbols for the whole of humanity.

25 All are possible. The important thing is to know what you think, and why, and to recognize the possibility that other interpretations may be equally valid.

4   Woman

3   **Clothes** – he says very little: only a 'cloth blown back from her face', and 'barefoot'. **Economic status** – nothing directly: we infer poverty from 'barefoot' and 'slums'. **Movements** – 'undulant grace', 'glides', 'not a ripple in her tread', 'erect'. **Karachi** – 'bazaar', 'stones, garbage excrement and crumbs of glass in the . . . slums'. **Himself** – he has a 'stoop'.

4   Her movements, and the Karachi slums.

6   **a)**   Some other country (see Authors, page 53).
  b)   One cannot be sure of this just by reading the poem, but the poet's observations suggest that he is an outsider.

7   The weight is a stone jar (line 4). It almost certainly has a secondary meaning, which is poverty, and the hard physical work it involves. A woman with servants would never have to carry weights on her head, and so would never learn to walk so erect and so gracefully.

8   'Hard work makes dignity' or 'Poverty creates beauty' are two possible morals.

9   **a)**   The answer depends on what moral you have chosen. Of the two given above, perhaps the first is more generally true than the second.
  c)   'Leisure makes dignity' or 'Hard work breaks people in the end' for the first; 'poverty creates ugliness' or 'wealth creates beauty' for the second.

10   **a)** Hearing, sight. **b)** she's dead. **c)** both are dead, and she 'clings' to the memory in the same way as the leaf clings to the threshold. **d)** No feelings are named, although the poem communicates sadness very effectively.

13   C.L.M. is Masefield's mother. No hints are given as to the man's age, but the last stanza suggests someone who has lived long enough to have a sense of failure and regret: he could be anything from 25 to 80.

14 Stanza Nos. 5 / 3 / 1 / 4 / 2.

15 a) Birth's releasing hell (24)
 b) Man's lust roves the world untamed (29)
 c) Unless my soul's face let her see / My sense of what she did for me (17-18)
 d) Men trample women's rights at will (23)
 e) Her beauty fed my common earth (4)
 f) Men triumph over women (27)
 g) Nor knock at dusty doors to find / Her beauty dusty in the mind (11-12)
 h) What woman's happier life repays / Her for those months of wretched days? (21-22)
 i) If the grave's gates could be undone (13)

16 a) The three women are described in largely different terms: the Sindhi woman is evoked by her graceful movements in contrast to squalid surroundings. Pound's woman by the things noticed in her absence and by the phrase 'she the rejoicer of the heart', and C.L.M. by her moral qualities. One might be tempted to claim a similarity in this matter of 'moral qualities' between Pound's woman (a 'rejoicer of the heart') and Masefield's mother, but look again at 'C.L.M.': there is no 'rejoicing' there.
 b) The poet does not present himself in 'Liu Ch'e'. In 'Sindhi Woman' and 'C.L.M.', the poets present themselves in a similar way: as contrasting, less dignified figures. Masefield makes the contrast much harsher, however: he is alive, and she is dead, he is guilty, and she was good. There is a moral and psychological depth here which is absent in the other poems.
 c) 'Liu Ch'e' has no moral. 'Sindhi Woman' makes a point about poverty and dignity (see question 8 above), and 'C.L.M.' seems to urge men to end their 'triumph over women' which is a completely different idea.
 d) All the poems treat women as a figure of respect, beauty and dignity. 'Liu Ch'e' and 'C.L.M.' add love, a term which 'C.L.M.' loads with moral qualities, especially self-sacrifice (in his mother's love for him) and guilt (in his love for her). It is perhaps worth noting that there is no hint of the erotic in these poems.

17 a) The Sindhi woman walks smoothly so that the jar will not fall from her head
 b) Pound uses symbols so as not to express emotion directly.
 c) In 'The Jewel Stairs' Grievance' the woman goes out to look for her lover.
 d) Masefield probably wrote C.L.M. to expiate feelings of guilt towards his mother

    e) He wants his mother to remain in the grave so that she cannot see how little he has done to thank her.

18 a) The Sindhi woman walks smoothly to prevent the jar falling from her head.

    b) Pound used symbols to avoid expressing emotion directly.

    e) He wants his mother to remain in the grave to prevent her seeing how little he has done to thank her.

19 Here are some of the many possible answers:

    a) They do this so that other people won't know if they are married or single.

    b) They do this so that they can work without worrying about their children.

    c) They do this to defend themselves in case they are attacked by a man.

    d) They do this to avoid male doctors. Or . . . to prevent men having medical control over their bodies.

    e) They do this so that men will stop looking at them as sex-objects.

    f) They do this to create equality in their homes.

    g) They do this to avoid being trapped. Or: to preserve their freedom.

    h) They do this to preserve their financial independence.

21 'Sindhi Woman': admiration, humility. Perhaps envy, surprise, compassion. 'Liu Ch'e': love, affection, nostalgia, sorrow. 'C.L.M.': love, admiration, humility, shame, guilt, sorrow, reverence, regret, embarrassment.

24 Both are by women. 'The Mutes' is by the American poet Denise Levertov, and 'Daphne Morse' is by Pamela Gillilan, who also wrote 'When You Died' (see Chapter 5). It is possible to guess the sex of the authors from evidence in the poems. There are certainly clues: 'The Mutes' describes a woman's mixed feelings of disgust and sexual pride in a way that suggests the author knows these feelings well and has observed them in herself; while 'Daphne Morse' describes a form of loving and exhilarated companionship which is completely untroubled by sexual feelings. Lines 21-25 strongly suggest the poet is female.

5   Love

1   **a)**   1 E;   2 C;   3 I;   4 D;   5 A;   6 G or H;   7 F;   8 B;   9 H or G.
    b)   Yes. For instance B – 6, 8 or 9
             C – 2 or 9
             D – 6, 8, 9 or even 5
             E – 2, 3, 6, 8 or 9
             G – 3, 4, 6 or 9
             H – 6, 8 or 9
             I – 3, 6, 8 or 9
    c)   There is also the concept of divine love (which can be seen as a religious version of 3, 4, 7 and 8); doing something 'for love' (meaning 'for no money'); and 'love' in games such as tennis, meaning 'zero'.
    d)   These could be discussed endlessly, but here is our verdict: Selfish: 2, 4, 5. Unselfish: 1, 3, 6, 7, 8, 9. Difficult to place: 2, 3, 6, 8, 9.

2   **a)**   night, the woods, you.
    b)   'you' (the lover).

3   He is irritated and frustrated. This is a well-known way of expressing petulance, and is (usually) not meant literally.

4   **a)**   A or D.   **b)**   A or D.   **c)**   C.

5   1-9, 10-22, 23-31, 32-36, 37.

6   **a)**   They offer solitude, peace and beauty, which produce a sense of 'knowing'.
    b)   This is a difficult question to answer precisely and objectively. It is partly a question of personal interpretation of lines 15-17 and 20-22. Our response would be: knowing what he feels and why he feels it, and that he can accept his feelings without too much pain.
    c)   This is almost certainly some cruelty or denial of love by the lover.
    d)   By offering solitude, peace, anonymity, rest . . .
    e)   It means he waited in suspense.
    f)   Again, this is difficult. The phrase suggests that the lover has ceased to cause him pain, but has joined the night and the woods in making him feel calm and happy.
    g)   The feet of an ignorant person.
    h)   This is the whole experience described in lines 10-22.
    i)   'Quack' is the noise that a duck makes. It suggests brainless, insensitive chatter.
    j)   See the answer to question 3 above.

7 a) The repeated words are: solitudes, and, dark, 'night and the woods and you', key, you, three, hour of knowing, flat, clear, you said, wood/woods, I wish. There are also repetitions of sound (rhymes) like 'part of the heart' and 'slowly . . . holy'.

   b) (iv).

   c) Both announce a change of rhythm and subject by creating a pause.

   d) Lines 1-9, with their regular metre and rhyme, aptly reflect the sense of safety and calm beauty in the evening. The short line 10 signals the change to a looser, less regular rhythm and rhyme-scheme, which echoes the exploratory sense of the words. Regularity returns after the interruption of line 23, but this time it is a crude 'crashing' rhythm suitable for the lover's insensitive behaviour.

8 All the following are possible:

   a) reverent, appreciative, calm

   b) turbulent, aggressive, condescending, dismissive, confused, irritable

   c) analytical, turbulent, confused.

10 Probably because these conventional public gestures seem painfully inadequate.

11 'Were you his wife?' expresses their relationship while he was alive. It is personal and unique to them. 'Are you the widow?' is an impersonal phrase which ignores the living relationship. The former is a reminder of her love, the latter a reminder of her loss.

12 Physical weakness, apathy, inertia, exhaustion.

13 Several explanations are possible. Here are some: cutting wild flowers to accompany the dead is an ancient custom with a powerful symbolic meaning; it is also a kind of revenge on nature for taking away a loved one; it is more personal than buying from a shop; it involves physical action (walking, searching, bending, picking, protecting) which can be comforting; it is more spontaneous, less conventionally decorative; the wild flowers of November are rare and therefore more precious than bought flowers.

14 The ironic phrase 'With customary thoughts / Of nature's mystical balance' suggests she will not scatter it among the roses. The most unusual and personal option ('shall I perhaps keep it') seems to interest her most.

15 'Rain' can sometimes be a symbol of fertility (see Philip Larkin's poem 'The Whitsun Weddings', Chapter 6), but more often in English writers (who see a lot of rain) it is a symbol of depression.
   'Wormy earth' suggests the burial of the dead.
   'Surviving' reminds us of its opposite: dead.
   'Thin metal': the fact that she mentions this suggests it surprised

her. In fact, vases are usually made of china and handsomely decorated. 'Thin metal' suggests something cheap, ugly, impersonal and unpleasantly functional.

'Ground bones . . .' again suggests a nasty surprise, contrary to the soft, pleasing 'silky ash' which she was expecting.

'Amazing skin' is a beautifully delicate announcement of physical love.

16 (iii). Free verse seems very well suited to this subject: partly because the poem is about feeling helpless in the face of grief, partly because it is presented as an honest, simple record of what happened. Rhyme and metre imply some degree of emotional and intellectual control, detachment and artifice.

17 A, C, E, G.

18 There are many. Grief, resentment, determination, disappointment, doubt, a sense of loss and of wasted beauty, admiration, emptiness about the future. One could certainly add more.

19 a) A gentleman asked if she was the widow.
   b) People asked why she did not follow the coffin.
   c) People asked why she did not have any funeral words spoken.
   d) People asked why she did not send flowers from a shop.
   e) She asked herself where she should put this substance.
   f) She asked herself if she should scatter it among the roses.
   g) She asked herself if she should disperse it into the winds.
   h) She reflected that they would have grown old together if he had lived, but now would not.

20 a) She drew his attention to the (beautiful) view.
   b) She remarked that it was nice to be alone a bit / She remarked how nice it was to be alone a bit.
   c) She observed that the days were drawing out.
   d) She pointed out that the sunset was pretty / She pointed out the prettiness of the sunset / She pointed out how pretty the sunset was.

21 a) Brooke seems to believe that there is magic in the woods.
   b) Brooke is sensitive to the colours and effects of the evening light.
   c) Brooke expects to find the key to his pain in the silence.
   d) Brooke describes his three loves growing into one.
   e) Brooke sees his lover's platitudes as an act of profanation.

22 a) Gillilan does not seem to believe that religion can help her.
   b) Gillilan is sensitive to the textures of the physical world.
   c) Gillilan does not expect to find consolation in anything.
   d) Gillilan describes in detail the experience of grief / Gillilan describes every detail of the experience of grief.
   e) Gillilan sees the death of her husband as a waste of something beautiful.

23 There are many possibilities. Here is one:
For Brooke, the lover's voice is a profanation, destroying the magic of the woods. He wants solitude and silence. His lover gives him only platitudes. For Gillilan, it is the voices of others that disturb her with their questions about flowers and funeral speeches. Both imply that silence is best at times of intense emotion.

24 a, b) The words, in order from silent to loud, are: *silence, hush, quietness, peace, swishing, crashing, voice, quacking, laughing, noise of a fool in mock distress, uproar.* (Note: the order could be varied for crashing/voice/quacking/laughing.)

    c) barely audible, faint/distant, soft, clear, loud, deafening, ear-splitting.

25 a) smash; **b)** crunch; **c)** rustle; **d)** splash; **e)** howl or roar; **f)** twitter; **g)** howl or roar; **h)** screech; **i)** drumming (possibly clatter); **j)** lapping; **k)** buzz; **l)** bang; **m)** creak; **n)** clatter; **o)** rumble.

26 a) Soothing: lapping, twitter; perhaps also rustle and buzz.

    b) Romantic: lapping, howl or roar (of wind), rumble; perhaps also drumming of rain and twitter of birds.
The differences in the two lists can be explained by the fact that bad weather (especially if it's violent) is often used to accompany scenes of passion in films and narrative. *Rustle* and *buzz* are not romantic because they are so businesslike; they are, however, quite soothing sounds.

28 Hushed, crashing, swishing, quacked.

31 The first claim, that 'to one mind' there was never a time of such quality before or after, is perfectly acceptable. It is quite usual for lovers to regard their own feelings as uniquely powerful. The second claim is untrue, judged by scientific standards, although it is, again, an understandable piece of passionate exaggeration.

    The philosophy of love expressed here is that love immortalises people (which in some cases is literally true, because it produces poetry which is read long after the lovers themselves have died. The classic expression of this in English is Shakespeare's Sonnet 18, 'Shall I compare thee to a summer's day?')

6   Trains

1   **b)**   Appreciation of the beauty of the scene; the harmony of the works of old man and nature; nostalgia for a more picturesque age (steam trains are now 'obsolete' in Britain, although they still run as a highly popular tourist attraction).

2   Sight and hearing.

3   Three aspects seem important here. 1) the immense speed, noise and mechanical power of an express-train (of which we are reminded by 'drew up' and 'the steam hissed'), which contrasts beautifully with the birdsong and surrounding stillness. 2) the poet is a passenger, so he does not choose to stop here, and the whole episode has that authentic feeling of a 'happy accident'. 3) the poet is purely an observer, without responsibility, free to indulge that especially receptive state of mind which train journeys alone seem to create (see question 24.)

6   **a)**   1. 1-10; 2. 11-20; 3. 21-57; 4. 58-71; 5. 71-80.
  b)   At the beginning (stanzas 1-2), and at the end (stanza 8)
  c)   (iii) and or (iv)

7   **a)**   them   (28) – the wedding-guests;
       their   (68) – the newly-married couples;
       it   (33) – the event;
       we   (71) – all the passengers on the train;
       it   (35) – the spectacle of the weddings;
       it   (75) – this frail travelling coincidence (the train and its passengers);
       they   (64) – the newly-married couples.
  b)   the people on the station platform.
  c)   'we' (the passengers) are loaded; 'they' are the people on the platform.

8   **a)**   'the tall heat that slept' (line 11)
  b)   'I thought of London . . . Its postal districts packed like squares of wheat' (69-70)
  c)   'bright knots of rail' (72)
  d)   'the secret like a happy funeral' (53)

9   **a)**   This is never stated, but probably refers to knowledge of what marriage means for a woman.
  b)   What has died is girlhood, innocence, virginity.
  c)   It is happy because marriage represents fulfilment, and the promise of a new generation.

10 This is the most obscure phrase in the poem. It helps to look at the context. The unmarried girls are fearful ('gripping their handbags tighter') as they see girls like them suddenly becoming wives. 'Wounding' refers to marriage, and has sexual and psychological connotations. It is 'religious' because it has just been blessed in church.

11 a) – d) The most important connotations to note here are those connected with (1) growth and fertility, (2) death. (The connections with 9 b) and c) above is evident.) It is, if you think about it, quite extraordinary that such contradictory ideas can co-exist successfully in the same image. **e)** An 'arrow-shower' would become a deadly rain. Yet somehow Larkin manages to maintain the suggestion of fertility – and therefore of hope.

14 This is a matter for personal interpretation. Larkin certainly allows the possibility of a religious significance, but does not press it. The power may simply be fertility, the power to have children. The couples are 'changed' by being married.

15 *Adlestrop*: one afternoon (2), it was late June (4), for that minute (13). *The Whitsun Weddings*: That Whitsun, late (1), not till about one-twenty on the sunlit Saturday (2-3), all afternoon (11), now and then (17), until (19), at first (21), once we started (27), and then (38), as we moved (48), while (54), at last (55), now (58), for some fifty minutes (59-60), in time (60), just long enough (61), never (67), this hour (68), as we raced (71), as the tightened brakes took hold (78).

16 a) one **b)** for, and then **c)** At first **d)** As/While **e)** at **f)** now and then **g)** until **h)** Not till **i)** while/as **j)** Once

17 a) in **b)** during **c)** While **d)** all **e)** before **f)** at **g)** over **h)** until **i)** in **j)** By **k)** while/when **l)** after **m)** earlier **n)** After **o)** for **p)** today **q)** in **r)** From **s)** to **t)** when.

18 a) in time **b)** at **c)** then **d)** when **e)** time **f)** in **g)** before **h)** After **i)** to **k)** early on **l)** in **m)** every **n)** At first.

20 getting away, pull out, ran, crossed, drifting, a slow and stopping curve southwards we kept, went by, dipped, rose, approached, stopped, started, passed, posed, go, waving, leant, climbed aboard, stood round, thrown, departing, hurried, shuffling, got under way, went past, running up, bowl, raced, standing, came close, loosed, slowed, took hold, swelled, falling, sent.

21 a)   rose, dipped, climbed, falling
   b)   getting away, pull out, stopped, started, go, departing, got under way
   c)   posed, waving, leant, stood
   d)   drifting, slow, slowed
   e)   ran, raced, hurried, running up
   f)   crossed, went by, approached, passed, came close, took hold, went past.

25 a) In this poem, as in 'The Whitsun Weddings', a train journey on a religious festival is used as an occasion for thoughts about people and what they are doing with their lives. Here the references to religious doctrine are explicit (Man of sorrows, Incarnation, the cross, etc) but deliberately rejected ('No, I shall think of Trevor'), whereas Larkin's references are implicit and neither rejected nor accepted.

b) The England of this poem is entirely desolate ('scrapyard Yorkshire', 'some even more desolate destination', 'the wind raged at his ankles'). Larkin's is more evenly balanced between beauty and ugliness.

c) The major difference is that this poem is about a meeting, whereas Larkin's people are only observed and their thoughts imagined. Steve Ellis clearly regards himself as having a more desirable life than Trevor, and there is a similar mixture of compassion and superiority in Larkin's descriptions of people.

d) 'The Whitsun Weddings' is a delicate mixture of both in relation to the whole of society. 'Man of Sorrows' is entirely about individuals, one a failure, the other not. Yet is Trevor entirely hopeless? Is his life intolerable to him?

26 a) About men and women, inhibition, missed opportunities.

b) Clearly the poet wants this poem to be read in relation to 'Adelstrop'. (In fact, 'Adlestrop' is such a famous poem that it is almost impossible for an English poet *not* to think of it while writing about trains.)

7   Culture

1 A: video rental shop, betting shop, amusement arcade, circus, discotheque, football stadium, striptease club, pub, motor racing track, bingo hall, funfair.
B: museum of science, theatre, arts centre, public library, art gallery, film club, university, archaeological museum, jazz club.
Note: public library, film club and jazz club could go in either category.

2 A: popular culture, or places of entertainment.
B: 'high' (or élite) culture.

3 It is generally assumed that B is 'better' than A because it is more intellectually stimulating, serious, complex, etc. On the other hand many people prefer A because it is more fun.

6 Masters: 'high' culture. Simpson: popular culture.

7 They are complementary.

8 a) I   **b)** the circulating library
c) those of you who could not see . . . (8)

9 The people of Spoon River.

10 c).

11 b).

12 Judging by the selling of the library and lines such as 'I am out of your way now, Spoon River,' he was unpopular.

13 a) False **b)** True **c)** False **d)** False **e)** True **f)** True **g)** False **h)** Partly true.

14 *Seth Compton:* which I built up for Spoon River, and managed for the good of inquiring minds / who could not see the virtue of knowing Volney's *Ruins* as well as Butler's *Analogy*, and *Faust* as well as *Evangeline* / who knows not what is evil / who knows not what is false.
Hubert's Museum: that I remember / who 'faced a firing squad, received 8 bullets through the body and head, yet LIVED!'

15 a) Circulating libraries, where the public borrowed books for a fee, were popular in Britain for 200 years and stimulated the self-education of the working classes.

   b) The first circulating library was set up in Edinburgh in 1726 by Allan Ramsay, a poet and bookseller, whose editions of medieval Scottish poetry and ballads contributed to the revival of Scottish vernacular poetry.

   c) Eighteenth century circulating libraries were often criticised for popularising light romantic novels, which were read largely by young women and considered improper.

   d) One of the most famous Nineteenth century circulating libraries was W H Smith's which was the predecessor of a well-known chain of stationers, newsagents and booksellers whose shops can be seen today in towns all over Britain.

   e) Another well-known library was Boot's, which was set up by the Nottingham businessman Jesse Boot in the late nineteenth century, and where the customers would ask for suggestions for books from specially-trained librarians.

   f) Circulating libraries, which remained popular in the 1920s and 1930s, declined after World War II and had all closed by 1970.

   g) The first public libraries in Britain, of which Canterbury (1847) was the earliest, opened in the 1840s and 1850s.

   h) London, whose first public library (Westminster) opened in 1857, did not have a second one until Wandsworth Public Library was opened in 1885.

   i) By 1900 there were 400 public libraries in Britain which were paid for by a small addition to the rates, to which some people objected.

   j) The American philanthropist Andrew Carnegie, who made his fortune from steel manufacturing and whose most famous saying is, 'the man who dies rich dies disgraced', gave enormous sums of money for public libraries in Britain and the USA.

k) By 1928 a public libraries service, which included children's libraries and village reading rooms, existed in most counties in Britain.

16 The first US library was the Harvard University Library which was founded in 1638 with money and 400 books from John Harvard, a Massachussetts priest. The first free lending libraries were founded by Thomas Bray, an English priest, in the late seventeenth century, although interest in them waned after Bray's death. The first successful public libraries were the subscription libraries which were founded by Benjamin Franklin and his friends in Philadelphia in 1731, under the name of The Library Company of Philadelphia. Members of this company, whose original collection still exists, paid a subscription in order to borrow books. Thomas Jefferson's library, which was bought from him in 1815, became the US Library of Congress – now the largest library in the world. The first public library paid for by taxes was founded in Peterborough, New Hampshire, in 1833. The idea, which was inspired by the ideal of free public education, spread quickly. In 1853 the first national convention of US librarians was held in New York. In 1876 Melvil Dewey published the Dewey Decimal Classification, a system of classifying books which is now in use all over the world. Between 1881 and 1919, the steel millionaire Andrew Carnegie helped to build 1,700 libraries in the USA. In the 20th century there has been a vast development of libraries and their services.

17 Suggested order from 'low' to 'high: moronic, crass, philistine, vulgar flashy, crude, simple, popular, sophisticated, complex, intellectual.

18

ADJECTIVE	NOUN (person)	NOUN (quality)
vulgar	#	vulgarity
sophisticated	sophisticate	sophistication
intellectual	intellectual	intellect
philistine	philistine	philistinism
crass	#	crassness
moronic	moron	#
popular	#	popularity
simple	simpleton*	simplicity
complex	#	complexity
intelligent	#	intelligence
flashy	#	flashiness
crude	#	crudity/crudeness
cheap	#	cheapness

*Note: 'simple' has two meanings – (1) the opposite of 'complex', (2) idiotic. 'Simpleton' expresses only (2), and means 'idiot'.

21 a) One is a 'radioactive swamp', in which civilization has been destroyed by nuclear holocaust, and mankind, suffering genetic mutations, is living in conditions of primitive squalor. The other is a 'plastic paradise' in which technology provides everything people need and yet is a kind of hell – presumably because life is too easy.

   b) Nuclear war, or peace.

22 One is crude heroic poetry, describing the past. The other is computer-generated political and religious propaganda.

23 **a)** Poets.

   b) The conquest of time and death. He is worried about the survival of poetry.

24 **a)**

25 Heath-Stubbs implies that our present civilization is a potential hell, in which humanity is at the mercy of technology – either from its physically destructive capacity (nuclear weapons), or from its psychologically destructive capacity (pointless gadgets). Whether you agree or not is likely to depend on your attitude to technology, and your view of human nature.

26 The attitude to culture is similar to that in 'Seth Compton', emphasising that high culture appeals to a minority and is backward-looking, or historically-based. (Note, however, that Heath-Stubbs does not claim, as Edgar Lee Masters does, that it also has an important role in education. Yet this assumption certainly lies behind Heath-Stubbs's poem too.)

8   Satire

4 Wright is attacking the cruelty of the way that we treat lobsters; and, by implication, perhaps the way we treat other edible animals.

5 **c)**

6 You can tell by the way he / Bobs about (16-17)
He'll love it (25)
you'll hear Mr Lobster laughing . . . to the grill (31-34)
Must be dead! (41)

7 'letting . . . mandibles clean' (62-65); 'pincers' (67); 'CLAW' (70); 'shell' (75).

8 The eater of the lobster is enjoying the results of his cruelty. The idea that he is turning into a lobster suggests that he will suffer similar cruelty at the hands of someone else.

9 b)

10 Complacency, snobbery, hypocrisy, racism, selfishness.

11 The woman in the first photograph, who is evidently rich.

12 The contradiction is between 'Gracious' (which implies gentleness, mercy, beauty and other life-giving qualities) and 'bomb the Germans'.

13 a) German women, me, our Empire, blacks and whites in the Forces, what our Nation stands for, 189 Cadogan Square.
   b) 1 me; 2 189 Cadogan Square; 3 what our Nation stands for; 4 our Empire; 5 whites in the Forces; 6 blacks in the Forces; 7 German women.

14 The requests are 'reserve for me a crown' and 'do not let my shares go down'. They are probably high on the scale (2 or 3).

15 Lines 28 and 42.

16 c)

17 a) no **b)** yes **c)** no **d)** yes **e)** no **f)** yes **g)** yes.

18 a) Lines 11-12, 23-24 and 30 suggest that she is selfish, though some of her other requests show that she is not *entirely* selfish. She does have some consideration for others.
   b) The contradiction in line 7 suggests stupidity, as does line 10 and the list of 'what our Nation stands for' (20-22).
   c) The two references to 'statesmen' (5, 39); 'class distinction' (21).
   d) Line 18.
   e) Stanza 5 in particular.
   f) Asking God to bomb the Germans but not her (7, 12); praying for herself and her property, yet offering to send white feathers to the cowards (12, 24, 30, 33).
   g) Line 24.
   h) This is the most difficult one to justify. Betjeman adds little touches of human weakness and sensitivity so that she does not seem a monster. Examples are lines 1-4, 8, 25, 35-36, 37-38, 41-42.

19 'know' and 'tell' are very flexible and useful words for making interpretations. They can be transitive or intransitive; they can be followed by a verb phrase ('you can tell he likes it'), a noun or a pronoun. After this comes 'by' or 'from', followed by a noun or a verb phrase beginning 'the way . . .' ('you can tell by the way he bobs about'). Other verbs are possible in place of 'tell': recognize, distinguish, see, hear, sense, etc. Questions are formed with *how* as in the exercise a)-g).

a) You can tell this by the use of the words 'screams', 'terror' and 'pain'.
b) You know this from words such as 'rockpool', 'mandibles', 'claw' and 'shell'.
c) You can tell from her address.
d) We know this from the request to 'bomb the Germans' and 'guide our Forces'.
e) We know she is conservative from the way she asks God to preserve the Empire and class distinction.
f) You can tell this by the way she asks God to protect the whites 'even more'.
g) You can tell this from lines such as 'Don't let anyone bomb me' and the final couplet.

20 b) This suggests that Kit Wright had a copy of this book in front of him as he wrote the poem.
c) This suggests that the recipe is sadistic.
d) This shows that Kit Wright was thinking of the eater as a wealthy person.
e) This shows that she is not completely selfish or heartless.
f) This shows that she is a conservative.
g) This means that she feels morally superior to those men who refuse to fight.
h) This suggests that she confuses religion with patriotism and snobbery.

21 a) dealing   b) including   c) sautéing   d) means   e) cut
f) cook g) do/face up to h) face up to/do i) suggest j) Run
k) Place l) covering m) hold n) Using o) cut p) join
q) killing r) plunge s) Remove t) cut.

22 Passage A is by Jane Grigson. The most significant differences are these:
1) in lines 6-15, Wright does not mention the RSPCA or that the gradual method of cooking is said to be painless; instead he says the lobster enjoys the experience.
2) 'weight the lid to stop the lobster jumping out' becomes 'stick a weight on the lid so he can't pop out!', which is more cheerfully colloquial. The lobster's attempts to get out are ironically interpreted as a sign of enjoyment (16-17).
3) Wright exploits the double meaning of 'cut up', and adds 'He'll love it' to reinforce the idea of the lobster enjoying itself.
4) 'No fooling with boiling and cooling': again the colloquial note (and rhyme).
5) 'winkle out the place ... carapace' adds a rhyme and suggests that the place will be difficult to find, therefore more of a struggle with the lobster, more of an invasion of its body.
6) 'whack' and 'smash' are added to suggest brutality..

23 a) The second prayer is more similar.
   b) spare, for his sake, they, O Lord, thy throne, gracious.

26 a) The excessive importance of money in human society.
   b) It is not a satire because there is no element of ridicule or irony (although there is a brief satirical moment in the line: 'Has he no money? Then let him eat dirt, and go cold.')

9   Cats and Dogs

1   Cats only: c, d, f, h, i, k, m, p, q, r, t, v, w, y.
Dogs only: a, b, e, g, j, l, o, s, u, x, z.
Both: n.

3   Whitworth: cats. Porter: dogs.

4   Whitworth: c. Porter: a.

5   Whitworth's poem seems to express a genuine love of cats (and possibly a genuine dislike of dogs). Porter's poem has dark political overtones (see 10 below), but remains very amusing.

6   **b)** Possibly **e)**.

7   Most of them are dishonest. See 8 below.

8   **a** 2   **b** 1   **c** 5   **d** 4   **e** 3

9   **a)** 1: lines 3, 10 (true of female dogs), 17, 22-23.
      2: 8-9 (the Greeks had no use for cats).
      4: 26-27.
   b) This is explained by the fact that a dog is speaking. The poem is a kind of political manifesto for dogs who hate cats.

10 A number of lines are reminiscent of racist propaganda employed by the Nazis in Germany from 1920 to 1945, and also of arguments used by more modern racists. The Nazi echoes are particularly strong in 'they stabbed us in the back last time' (a reference to the humiliation of Germany by the Versailles Treaty of 1919) and 'The Rule of Dogs shall last a thousand years!' (a similar boast was made by Hitler.)

11 Dogs. This is an assumed voice.

12 *Mort aux Chats*   *Max's Verse*
   Lines 2-3, 17   Line 3
   Lines 22-23   Lines 7, 9-10

13 One might describe lines 15-16 as type 4.

14 a) This would have made the idea of shooting them sound vicious and inhuman.
   b) graceful, delight.

15 a) This is to stress the antiquity of man's affection for cats, and to create a mystical, distancing atmosphere around them.
b) 'shot on sight' sounds brutally modern in this context.

16 spread infection, pollute the air, decadent societies, had no use for, harrowing, unbearably, alien, smell, too much, stabbed us in the back, there have never been any great artists who were, they don't deserve, I blame, why should they insist . . .?, who needs to . . .? death to.

20 *Max's Verse:*
delicate: definitions 1 and 2.
nature: definition 2.
Mort aux Chats:
all right: definition 2.
rule: definition 3.
help: definition 3.

21 a) delight   **b)** delicate/subtle   **c)** brave   **d)** graceful
e) foolhardiness **f)** clean **g)** secretive **h)** subtle/delicate

22

ADJECTIVE	NOUN (quality/thing)	NOUN (person)	VERB
infectious	infection	#	infect
polluting	pollution	polluter	pollute
#	consumption	consumer	consume
fond	fondness	#	#
traditional	tradition	traditionalist	#
sleepy	sleep	sleeper	sleep
stormy	storm	#	storm
great	greatness	#*	#
artistic	art/artistry	artist	#
linguistic	language	linguist	#
religious	religion	#	#
graceful	grace	#	#
delicate	delicacy	#	#
secretive	secretiveness	#	#
clean	cleanliness	cleaner	clean
personal	personality	person	personalize
delightful	delight	#	delight
brave	bravery	#*	brave
favoured/favourite	favour	favourite	favour
poetic	poem/poetry	poet	#
wise	wisdom	#*	#
true	truth	#	#
subtle	subtlety	#	#

* These (and certain other) adjectives can be used to form plural collective nouns by prefixing 'the': 'the great', 'the good', 'the brave', 'the poor', 'the wise' and so on. Here are some examples: 'Fortune aids the brave' (Terence); 'the land of the free, the home of the brave' (US national anthem); 'Let me smile with the wise, and feed with the rich' (Samuel Johnson).

23 a) grace   **b)** delicacy   **c)** secretiveness   **d)** cleanliness
e) fond   **f)** favourites   **g)** delight   **h)** truth   **i)** wise
j) traditional **k)** poetic **l)** linguistic **m)** sleep **n)** subtlety/
artistry   **o)** personal   **p)** stormy   **q)** infectious   **r)** pollution
s) consumption **t)** religious.

28 The suggestion is that dogs are privileged creatures in England. It
has also been claimed that this is an allegory of political freedom
in England.

10   City life

2/3 a) Illinois **b)** temperate   **c)** 1837   **d)** 3 million   **e)** on a lake
f) metal and food   **g)** unskilled immigrants, crime   **h)** gangsters.

5   Pride

6   NOUNS: toolmaker, stacker of wheat, player, freight handler,
shoulders, head, slugger, mouth, teeth, wrist, ribs.
ADJECTIVES: wicked, crooked, brutal, proud, alive, coarse,
strong, cunning, tall, bold, fierce, bareheaded, half-naked.
VERBS: singing, flinging, shoveling, wrecking, planning, building,
breaking, rebuilding, laughing, bragging, sweating.

7   **a)** real. **b)** prostitutes. **c)** prostitutes (this is debatable) and
gunmen. **d)** 'During the 1920s . . . lived down' (paragraph 6) –
gunmen; 'Since the 1940s . . . Asian families' and 'About a
fourth . . . welfare aid' (paragraph 7) – poor women and
children. **e)** To present an accurate and balanced picture; so as
not to be accused of idealizing the city.

8   **d)**

10   anguish, despair, dislike.

11   **a)** it pounds men down past humbleness (6-7)
b) it's a gentle and undemanding planet, even here. (40-41)

13   **a)** 1-10   **b)** 11-16   **c)** 17-21   **d)** 22-27   **e)** 28-39   **f)** 40-50
g) 51-57/8   **h)** 58/9-63.

14   **a)** True   **b)** False   **c)** False   **d)** False   **e)** True   **f)** False
g) True **h)** True **i)** False **j)** True.

15   It is blind because it cannot see what it is doing. The word
suggests moral blindness too. It is red because it is fiery. The
similarity with a rhinoceros is suggested by its bulk, its
momentum, its wildness, its monster-like appearance.

16   could (1), cannot (5), can (10), could (28), can't (44, 45), can't
(58).

17 a) They stoop at 35 possibly cringing from the heavy and terrible sky. (7-9)

   b) In the mills and refineries of its south side Chicago passes its natural gas in flames bouncing like bunsens from stacks a hundred feet high. (11-13)

   c) The stench stabs at your eyeballs. (14)

   d) Sievers, whose old man spent most of his life in there, remembers a 'nigger in a red T-shirt pissing into the black sand.' (24-27)

   e) It does no good appealing to some ill-invented Thunderer (45-46)

18 a) Here [or It's a place where] you can understand why the Bible is the way it is.

   b) I found a farm where I could shoot pheasant.

   c) You could see the feeding rings of fish 100 yards away.

   d) You can't blame anybody else.

   e) It can only exist if we allow it to. / It can only exist on our sufferance.

   f) Nobody can stand against this. / Nobody will ever be able to stand against this.

   g) A small part of it could die if I weren't around.

20 You should use the following words to describe the poem: concise, memorable, punchy, striking. The other words are more suitable for the article.

21 a) Chicago has the world's . . . largest grain market (paragraph 3). Trucks and railroad cars carry more goods in and out of Chicago than in and out of any other city in the United States (paragraph 2).

   b) See 20 above.

23 Lawrence's poem is written by a man who has done what Welch says he intends to do — 'walk away from it'. But Lawrence points out that even if you walk away, the 'living death' of your fellow men still affects you. Welch might well answer that walking away is still a great deal better than staying.